W9-BCI-564

Many Paths

FAITH MEETS FAITH

An Orbis Series in Interreligious Dialogue

Paul F. Knitter, General Editor

In our contemporary world, the many religions and spiritualities stand in need of greater intercommunication and cooperation. More than ever before, they must speak to, learn from, and work with each other, in order to maintain their own identity and vitality and so to contribute to fashioning a better world.

FAITH MEETS FAITH seeks to promote interreligious dialogue by providing an open forum for the exchanges between and among followers of different religious paths. While the series wants to encourage creative and bold responses to the new questions of pluralism confronting religious persons today, it also recognizes the present plurality of perspectives concerning the methods and content of interreligious dialogue.

This series, therefore, does not want to endorse any one school of thought. By making available to both the scholarly community and the general public works that represent a variety of religious and methodological viewpoints, FAITH MEETS FAITH hopes to foster and focus the emerging encounter among the religions of the world.

Already published:

Toward a Universal Theology of Religion, Leonard Swindler, Editor
The Myth of Christian Uniqueness, John Hick and Paul F. Knitter, Editors
An Asian Theology of Liberation, Aloysius Pieris, S.J.
The Dialogical Imperative, David Lochhead
Love Meets Wisdom, Aloysius Pieris, S.J.

FAITH MEETS FAITH SERIES

Many Paths

A Catholic Approach to Religious Pluralism

Eugene Hillman, C.S.Sp.

ORBIS BOOKS
Maryknoll, New York 10545

The Catholic Foreign Mission Society of America (Maryknoll) recruits and trains people for overseas missionary service. Through Orbis Books, Maryknoll aims to foster the international dialogue that is essential to mission. The books published, however, reflect the opinions of their authors and are not meant to represent the official position of the society.

Copyright © 1989 by Eugene Hillman, C.S.Sp
Published by Orbis Books, Maryknoll, NY 10545
Manufactured in the United States of America

Manuscript Editor and Indexer: Joan Marie Laflamme

Library of Congress Cataloging-in-Publication Data

Hillman. Eugene.
    Many paths: a Catholic approach to religious pluralism/Eugene Hillman
        p.   cm. — (Faith meets faith)
    Bibliography: p.
    Includes index.
    ISBN 0-88344-547-6.   — ISBN 0-88344-548-4 (pbk.)
    1. Christianity and other religions. 2. Religous pluralism —
Christianity. 3. Catholic Church — Relations. 4.Catholic Church —
Doctrines. I. Title. II. Series.
    BR127.H56 1989
261.2 — dc19
                                  88-37470
                                     CIP

We explain the fact that the Milky Way is there by the doctrine of creation, but how do we explain the fact that the Bhagavad Gita is there?

—Wilfred Cantwell Smith

Contents

Preface

My interest in the theological relationship between Christianity and the other religions dates back to the early 1950s when I was sent, as the first Catholic missionary, to the Maasai people of northern Tanganyika Territory (now Tanzania). While attempting to understand the culture and history of these people, with a view to "converting" some of them to a Roman Catholic version of Christianity and thereby establishing among them an initial base for the gradual development of a self-propagating replica of the Roman Catholic Church, I became increasingly troubled by my own recurring questions about my relevance to their needs, specifically, whether and to what extent they really needed the historically conditioned and culturally alien religious experience of Europeans and North Americans. The questions became acute in proportion as I came to appreciate the balanced and culturally integrated nature of their own religious experiences, beliefs, practices and celebrations.

To find some answers, I searched the few available works of theology concerned with cross-cultural missionary activity. Seeking more contemporary answers, I also wrote inquiring letters to notable theologians. Karl Rahner, Edward Schillebeeckx, Piet Fransen and Bernard Häring gave me lengthy and enlightening replies. Father Rahner even invited me to spend some days discussing these questions with him in Freiburg im Breisgau between the first and second session of the Second Vatican Council. These informal discussions encouraged me to publish *The Church as Mission* in 1965. Further missionary experience, reflection and study led to the publication of *The Wider Ecumenism* three years later and *Polygamy Reconsidered* in 1975. The major themes of these books, further elaborated in the light of more recent studies, are variously brought together in the present volume.

For the human support and theological education given to me over the years, an expression of gratitude is due in the very first place to the Maasai people who taught me the meaning of religious pluralism and demonstrated in their lives that God's grace is not less operative among non-Christians than it is among Christians. Second, I am grateful to the distinguished theologians cited above for the help and encouragement they gave me in their generous replies to my many questions. Finally, I wish also to thank those who, after reading critically the chapters of the present volume, offered me valuable suggestions and indispensable corrections: Lucien Richard of Weston School of Theology in Cambridge, Gavin D'Costa of the West London Institute of Higher Education, Paul Knitter of Xavier University in Cincinnati, John Coakley and Sheila Megley of Salve Regina— The Newport College in Rhode Island.

Since it is not possible for one person, much less in a single volume, to say everything that could or should be said about the emerging Christian theology of religion, the limited aim here is to set forth the general lines and contemporary orientation of the Roman Catholic contribution to this rapidly developing area of theological reflection. Most Christian theologians would probably agree that Roman Catholics have been among the pioneers in this field and that Karl Rahner has been a singular trail blazer.

Such is the warrant for the present effort to articulate, from one particular vantage point, a credible theological approach to interreligious dialogue. This wider ecumenism to which Christians were summoned by the Second Vatican Council may prove to be, because of its far-reaching implications, the Council's most revolutionary act. If this summons is taken seriously by increasing numbers of theologians, pastors and missionaries, we may expect the self-understanding of Christians to be profoundly enriched, and the church's missionary outreach to be extensively transformed.

The first chapter is concerned with the significance of religion as experienced by human beings in their respective historico-cultural situations. The second chapter traces the historical development of Christian thought regarding the actual meaning of God's loving proximity to the whole of humankind. The third chapter looks at the implications of the foregoing as bases for a new Christian theological interpretation of non-Christian religions and for a trusting participation in interreligious dialogue worldwide. The final chapter argues that the reconciliation of this wider ecumenism with the Christian world mission is possible only through a radically renewed understanding of Christianity's traditional missionary ministry among the followers of other religions.

These chapters were written consecutively, each being a presupposition to those that follow. It is suggested they be read in the same sequence.

Abbreviations

The following abbreviations are used in reference to ecclesiastical documents, works of Thomas Aquinas and Karl Rahner:

AC   "Atheism and Implicit Christianity." Karl Rahner (1968).

AG   *Ad Gentes*. Vatican II, "Decree on the Church's Missionary Activity" (1965).

CF   *The Christian of the Future*. Karl Rahner (1967).

CT   *Catechesi Tradendae*. Pope John Paul II, "Catechesis in Our Time" (1971).

DA   "Discourse at All-Africa Episcopal Conference." Pope Paul VI (1969).

DH   *Dignitatis Humanae*. Vatican II, "Declaration on Religious Liberty" (1965).

EA   "Evangelization in Africa Today." Pope Paul VI (1975).

EN   *Evangelii Nuntiandi*. Paul VI, "Evangelization in the Modern World" (1975).

FC   *Foundations of Christian Faith*. Karl Rahner (1978).

GS   *Gaudium et Spes*. Vatican II, "Pastoral Constitution on the Church in the Modern World" (1965).

LG   *Lumen Gentium*. Vatican II, "Dogmatic Constitution on the Church" (1965).

MG   *Mission and Grace*. Karl Rahner (1963).

NA   *Nostra Aetate*. Vatican II, "Declaration on the Relation of the Church to Non-Christian Religions" (1965).

NG   *Nature and Grace*. Karl Rahner (1963).

RH   *Redemptor Hominis*. John Paul II, "The Redeemer of Humankind" (1979).

SM   *Sacramentum Mundi: An Encyclopedia of Theology*. Karl Rahner, ed. (1968).

ST   *Summa Theologica*. St Thomas Aquinas (1947).

TI   *Theological Investigations*. Karl Rahner (1961–81).

UR   *Unitatis Redintegratio*. Vatican II, "Decree on Ecumenism" (1964).

1

Religion: A Component of Culture

Any effort to construct a theology of religions must obviously be grounded in sound anthropology. As preliminaries to all that follows in this book, therefore, some historical and anthropological reflections are offered here on the significance of religion and its place in the lives of real people who experience life and seek its meaning always and only within a specific historical time frame and cultural context. Within these boundaries of tangible human experience, religions appear almost everywhere as elements integrated, in much the same way as languages, within particular cultures, each one having its own characteristic ethos and limited world view. Another preliminary point made in this chapter relates anthropology and theology. Here and in the subsequent chapters the theological term *faith* is understood as distinct from, but related to, religious belief.

CULTURAL ARROGANCE

The impact of Western technology and commercialism in areas colonized for generations by competitive European powers—with significant help from the rifle and the Maxim gun—fostered the ethnocentric illusion that Western cultures were superior to all others. This fiction was conveniently reinforced in the nineteenth century by the pseudoscientific hypotheses of Social Darwinism. It was assumed that the "backward" ways of colonized peoples would eventually be superseded by Western ways of being human and religious. It was supposed that, together with much else in their cultures, the countless religions of humankind's vast majority, living outside of Europe and North America, were destined for the scrap heap of history. The sentiments of United States Senator Albert J. Beveridge may be taken as fairly typical of Western cultural arrogance around the turn of the century:

God has not been preparing the English speaking and Teutonic peoples for a thousand years for nothing. . . . He made us master organ-

1

izers of the world to establish system where chaos reigned. He has given us the spirit of progress to overwhelm the forces of reaction throughout the earth. He has made us adept in government that we may administer government among savage and senile peoples. Were it not for such a force as this the world would relapse into barbarism and night. And of all our race He has marked the American people as His chosen nation to finally lead in the redemption of the world (quoted in Bellah 1975:83).

Such sentiments are rarely proclaimed today outside of neo-Nazi circles. But they still manifest themselves occasionally by a slip of the tongue or in the diplomatic double talk of some European and American policymakers and ecclesiastical functionaries. These sentiments, alas, have a long history in the hearts of Western peoples, not only among Senator Beveridge's Anglos and Teutons but also among the beneficiaries of the French, Belgian, Dutch and Iberian commercial adventurers and conquistadors who for centuries plundered the lands of other peoples.

The distinguished historian of religion Wilfred Cantwell Smith was right when he remarked "that the fundamental flaw of Western civilization in its role in world history is arrogance, and that this has infected also the Christian Church." The history of colonialism, not easily separated from the history of the expansion of Christianity, contains ample evidence to support such a statement. Anyone who feels that this criticism is unwarranted is urged by Professor Smith to "ask any Jew, or read between the lines of the works of modern African and Asian thinkers" (Smith 1972:130). Southern Baptist Old Testament scholar Burlan A. Sizemore, Jr., put it this way:

The supercilious condescension with which the Christian often sweeps aside the faith claims of others in an alleged comparative study, but in which the Christian has no appreciation for the subjective faith experience of the other, is inexcusable arrogance (Sizemore 1976:416).

PEJORATIVE TERMINOLOGY

The early anthropologists, in studying foreign cultures and alien religions, were contaminated by an unwarranted evolutionary cast of thought, spellbound perhaps by Herbert Spencer's dictum, "From the simple to the complex." Andrew Lang, for example, spoke of "high gods and low races," while Edward Burnett Tyler wrote about "religion from that of savages up to that of civilized man." Many examples of the shabby treatment of traditional African religions by Western scholars are cited in an angry but well-documented book by the Uganda poet Okot p'Bitek who urges, among other things, the banishing of such "meaningless" and "nuisance" terms as "fetishism" and "animism," which were "coined and used by Western writers in their imaginary speculation" (p'Bitek 1970:105; cf. James 1958:9–27; Berger 1970:45,73–79). These scholars were perched on the highest rungs of an evolutionary ladder, fabricated by their own imaginations, which lent an aura of scientific plausibility to their ethnocentrism.

The term *primitive* is no less offensive when used to designate the cultures or religions of contemporary preliterate peoples who are, in fact, no closer to the origins of the human enterprise than modern Europeans and North Americans. All are equally distant from those remote beginnings, and just as near to the end of the journey as populations uncritically assumed to be more "advanced." Claude Levi-Strauss offers this relevant comment:

So-called primitive societies, of course, exist in history; their past is as old as ours, since it goes back to the origin of the species. Over thousands of years they have undergone all sorts of transformations. . . . But they have specialized in ways different from those which we have chosen. Perhaps they have in certain respects remained closer to very ancient conditions of life, but this does not preclude the possibility that in other respects they are further from these conditions than we are (Levi-Strauss 1967:46).

CLASSICISM

The pejorative labelling of alien peoples betrays an attitude deeply rooted in Western culture. Bernard Lonergan exposed these roots in his critical analysis of what he calls the "classicist mentality." This is a way of viewing reality and stabilizing it in immutably universal concepts from which deductions are then made and conceptual categories fashioned to cover everything. The principles, from which this static conceptual order of reality flows, are traced by Lonergan to Aristotle. They are embodied in the classical education of the Western tradition. In the words of Lonergan:

It was a matter of acquiring and assimilating the tastes and skills, the ideals, virtues and ideas, that were pressed upon one in a good home and through a curriculum in the liberal arts. This notion, of course, had a very ancient lineage. It stemmed out of the Greek *paideia* and Roman *doctrinae studium atque humanitatis*, out of the exuberance of the Renaissance and its pruning in the Counter-Reformation schools of the Jesuits. Essentially it was a normative rather than an empirical notion of culture, a matter of models to be imitated, or ideal characters to be emulated, of eternal verities and universally valid laws (Lonergan 1974:101).

For more than two millennia the classicist view dominated the European understanding of reality; it is still a factor in the thinking not only of Western peoples but also of many others resocialized or "Westernized" under the influence of colonialism. Classicism was the opposite of barbarism. People were humanized, developed or civilized to the extent that they learned to approximate the models and ideals produced and articulated by the cultural genius of Western peoples. Missionaries, imbued with these ideals and formed according to these models, sent out from Europe and North America to evangelize "barbarous" or "primitive" peoples, would have no qualms about imposing their own culture as a precondition for admission through baptism into the Christian community. They would do this in the name of God, imagining they were conferring "the double benefit of both the true religion and the true culture" (Lonergan 1972:363).

By conceiving Western culture in normative and universal terms, it was almost inevitable that the Western heritage should appear to be the one and only really humanizing or civilizing culture, the one most appropriate for all human beings and most compatible with "the true religion." Not surprisingly, this culture was also seen as the one norm against which all other cultures could be evaluated on a scale of higher and lower, primitive or advanced, backward or progressive (cf. Lonergan 1974:93). Ernst Troeltsch even took the culture of Europe as a norm for validating Christianity which, he said, "could not be the religion of such a highly developed racial group if it did not possess a mighty power and truth." In this view, Christianity is so "indissolubly bound up with elements of the ancient and modern civilization of Europe" that it "stands or falls" with this particular civilization. So the wearing of Western cultural garb by the "less developed races" is a precondition for their encounter in faith with Christ (Troeltsch 1923:24). As Hilaire Belloc expressed it, "Europe is the faith; the faith is Europe" (Belloc 1920:331).

Although the classicist recognizes that varied circumstances cause alterations, these are regarded as merely accidental changes not touching the substance or kernel or root of things assumed to be stable, immutable, fixed. Such a mentality is hardly compatible with the pluralist notion of culture arising from the empirical observations of modern anthropologists living among the peoples they study. In chapter 4 we will look at some of the mischief done in the past, and continued today, through the ethnocentrism of the "classicist mentality."

THE EMPIRICAL NOTION OF CULTURE AND RELIGION

The notion of culture, as generally understood today in the social sciences, embraces everything created by human beings and handed on from generation to generation. Each generation learns from previous ones how to be human. The inheritors learn to adapt their heritage of knowledge and skills to the contingencies and peculiarities of their particular time and place in the human continuum. As an elementary definition, we may say that culture consists of all learned behavior; it includes all the knowledge handed down from one generation to another and all the ways of behaving learned from others; it is somewhat similar to, but sharply distinguished from, genetically programmed knowledge and behavior.

In the realms of freedom and intellection that distinguish human beings from all other mammals, cultures are external sources of essential information; they are analogous to genes determining, from within, the foundational shapes and functions of organisms. It is through one's culture that one's ability to deliberate is developed in the course of asking relevant questions, reflecting upon available data, and integrating answers that satisfy intelligence and speak to the heart (cf. Lonergan 1957:236). Every human act, in other words, is culturally and historically conditioned. Not only external behavior but every innermost thought, feeling and judgment is formed and shaped and colored by the peculiarity of a person's circumscribed cultural context and limited historical vantage point. In Lonergan's succinct definition, "a culture is a set of meanings and values informing a common way of life, and there are as many cultures as there are distinct sets of such meanings and values" (Lonergan 1972:301; 1974:91).

In his persuasive analysis of culture, anthropologist Clifford Geertz describes culture patterns in terms of blueprints or recipes functioning in the common human world of intersubjectivity. These patterns, like strands of DNA, form coded programs "for the institutions of the social and psychological processes which shape public behavior" (Geertz 1973:92). This patterned public behavior, in turn, socializes newborn members of the ethnic community and resocializes immigrants from other ethnic-culture societies, teaching them how they are expected to think, feel and act as human beings. Cultures do not, however, determine or condition us in the same way as genes. Profoundly and extensively influential, even unavoidable, as they are, culture patterns do not negate the human freedom to rebel and to change the patterns or to borrow patterns invented by other peoples in different times and places. Human creativity reigns over cultures.

Religions, like languages, are cultural inventions; they are human-made and handed on from generation to generation. As products of human creativity, religious forms, structures, rites and beliefs are variously modified as they are appropriated and reassessed by subsequent generations borrowing continuously and sometimes extensively from both the creativity of their own respective generations and from the genius of other peoples. Human beings become religious in a manner similar to their achieving fluency in a language. For most people both religious sensitivity and linguistic proficiency develop gradually without much self-conscious reflection or close scrutiny. For most people the religions they follow, like the languages they call their own, are determined for them by their place of birth and by obscure political events in the remote historical past of their progenitors. In such matters, as Pascal said, "a meridian decides" what is appropriate. On the other side of that imaginary line there is usually another religion and different language.

SOCIALIZATION

It is commonly and uncritically assumed during childhood that one's particular religion and one's language are simply givens of the human condition. It is something of a discovery, even shocking for some, to learn that there are numerous other religions and languages not only quite different from their own but also incomprehensible to one another. It is even surprising to learn that in one's own country significant differences exist in the practice of religion and in the verbalization of language. Such discoveries expand human consciousness as they raise questions about the different religious and linguistic heritages. The thoughtful child begins to wonder why these differences exist and what they mean, whether and to what extent his or her own heritage is really right or adequate, superior or inferior to that of others. A sense of relativity awakens at an early age together with an incipient recognition of cultural pluriformity.

For the questions of children, however, there are always dogmatic answers at hand in the cultural world of their parents and their elder siblings, answers fashioned during countless generations and representing the "wisdom of the ages." The answers, often most impressive, if sometimes tediously complex, tend to still the questioning. Forms of schooling and religious instruction also provide numbing answers, even before the corresponding questions have arisen in growing minds. Consult, for examples, a traditional Sunday School catechism.

Such schooling, by promoting conformity in thought and behavior while cautioning against critical reflection and originality, reinforces the validity of the inherited world view. Everything, then, seems to hold together more or less. So most people can go on with the business of living without experiencing much need for further philosophical inquiry into the meaning of their heritage of things, customs, conventions, styles, gestures, practices, values, mores, tastes, beliefs, rituals, structures and systems. Through gradual internalization these cultural realities become "natural" and "normal" to the new members as they are progressively socialized into their particular communities of destiny. These members are thus inclined to become prisoners of their respective cultures. They are easily blinded to the common humanity reflected in the "strange ways" and "odd customs" of other peoples.

ETHNOCENTRISM

A cultural heritage is necessary for each human being, enabling the person rationally and freely to encounter and interpret reality; it is necessary in the way that a spider needs the web of its own creation. We depend upon our cultural heritage, our web, so totally that we can hardly function humanly without it. We understand and express ourselves best in its terms. Inevitably, like the "classicists" mentioned already, we tend to judge pejoratively the ways of other peoples whose historical situations and cultural matrices are very different from our own. We are inclined to judge other peoples only in the light of the historical experiences of our own people and according to the values emphasized and the norms developed within, and for the purposes of, our own historico-cultural world. While eating eggs ourselves, we find it abnormal that others prefer grubs. The issue is not really what is eaten, but what our cultures tell us about eating. Again we are reminded of the problem discussed by sociologists and anthropologists under the heading of ethnocentrism. This worldwide human affliction is both congenital and chronic, but not completely incurable.

When it comes to religions, the reality of ethnocentrism may be expressed in these words of Xenophanes of Colophon (c. 530 B.C.): "Aethiopians have gods with snub-noses and black hair; Thracians have gods with grey eyes and red hair" (quoted in Freeman 1948:22). Each ethnic-culture group tends to see its own religion as superior; some hold their gods to be exclusively authentic, thus demanding that all peoples bow down before them. The religions are seen as the appropriate instruments for getting people to behave in ways that please the gods, even when the notion of divinity is not sharply focused.

The religions need to develop the requisite forms, structures, systems, rules, rituals, customs, practices, teachings and beliefs relevant to their goals. More often than not they also get involved in politics, ethics, aesthetics, education, law and economics. All these developments, whether progressive or retrogressive, are accomplished gradually by successive generations in the same historical way that languages are constructed and continue to change with the times. The English language is not today what it was in the days of Chaucer, nor is the religion of the English-speaking peoples.

IDEOLOGY

Ideologies emerge in support of each religion. An ideology is a simplified set of ideas, concepts, theories, hypotheses and biases reflecting and supporting the needs, interests, values, doctrines, beliefs and prejudices of a particular group, class, culture, tribe or nation. An ideology provides a convenient frame of reference for interpreting the meaning of events, especially new ones, fitting them into a general pattern of plausibility.

Fundamentalist Protestants with vested interests in slavery, for example, used selected texts of the Bible ideologically to show the compatibility of that socioeconomic institution with Christianity. Their critics could then be dismissed as mere humanists, if not agents of Satan. Fundamentalist Catholics used selected ecclesiastical teachings in the same literalistic way to support their own culturally and historically conditioned view of Christianity when radical theologians questioned the morality of salvery. Because of their ideologically different perceptions of Christianity, however, and in spite of their similar methods of seeking religious truth, these same Protestants and Catholics tended to see each other as lost sheep. They were not, usually, keen supporters of an ecumenical dialogue among separated Christian communities; much less were they promoters of the wider ecumenism of interreligious dialogue.

Even today fundamentalists, whether Catholic or Protestant, find it hard to accept the new perspectives introduced by scholars using modern methods of historical criticism for interpreting biblical texts and ecclesiastical documents. Fundamentalists, preferring literalistic interpretations, resist innovations and cling to their ideologies in an effort to hold together, unchanged, the inherited world view of their respective groups in the face of the phenomena of constant historical change and invincible cultural pluralism. Change and pluralism are perceived as threats to the inherited opinions, structures and systems that have served them well since childhood, providing clear and comforting answers to the perplexing questions of life.

Ideologies thus tend to close a group in upon itself as a way of maintaining the feelings of security and stability provided by an unalterable viewpoint in matters of great importance. Ideologies also help to support the vested interests of persons in power and to protect the interests of those with something to lose if the status quo should be significantly upset. The exporters of military equipment, for example, are not likely to be enthusiasts for negotiated solutions to disputes among their customers. Neither are international bankers whose usurious loans enable their clients to purchase the military hardware used to keep ruling elites in power.

It is not only in the political and religious realms that the negative aspects of ideologies are manifest. They show themselves also wherever decisions are made with little regard for reliable data or sober reasoning that might contradict or even question the dominant ideological presuppositions. Even the most dire consequences, however predictable in the long-term, tend to be obsured by a rigid ideological focus. Military history is replete with examples of ideologically generated disasters, for example, Verdun, Stalingrad, Dresden. In recent years a number of major American business enterprises have radically compromised their own long-term interests through a single-minded commitment to a profit-maximizing ideology that usually works only in the short term, for example, Johns Manville, Continental Illinois Bank, E. F. Hutton (cf. Gellerman 1986:85–90). More than any corporate managers, however, religious ideologues—through their holy wars, crusades and witch hunts—have brought devastation upon their flocks.

Ideologies surely have much to do with the folly, perversity and woodenheadedness amply illustrated, from Troy to Vietnam, in Barbara Tuchman's book about "a phenomenon noticeable throughout history regardless of place or period: the pursuit by governments of policies contrary to their own interests" (Tuchman 1984:4), at least in the long term. Therefore, if people fail to look critically from time to time at themselves and their convenient support systems, they are apt to become trapped in their own ideologies, which then become propaganda believed by themselves more than by others. Ideologies have their social purposes and can save us a lot of time that otherwise might be needed for research and reflection on hard data. But ideologies can also be as self-destructive for a nation, an army, a corporation or a religious institution as Captain Ahab's ideas and feelings about Moby Dick were for Ahab and his hapless crew.

COMMUNICATING MEANING

Change and pluralism are generally accepted in the realm of languages. When it comes to religions, however, they are often resisted. Yet both of these cultural realities, language and religion, are similar; they are humanly invented systems of symbols that both constitute and communicate meanings. Languages do this through the articulation and codification of meaningful sounds developed as a collaborative effort within a common field of human experience. Religions do this through the joint creation of social structures, myths and rituals. By means of such symbols people learn to communicate and convey meanings to other persons.

Commonly shared meanings bind people together in communities. These groups transmit to successive generations the meanings that clarify or obscure, reform or deform, enrich or impoverish, the common meanings and understandings required for the coherence and perseverance of communities. Human communities are not, therefore, just aggregates of individuals living in the same geographical location. Bernard Lonergan explains all of this at length in his treatment of community as "an achievement of common meaning." In Lonergan's words:

Common meaning is potential when there is a common field of experience, and to withdraw from that common field is to get out of touch. Common meaning is formal when there is common understanding, and one withdraws from that common understanding by misunderstanding, by incomprehension, by mutual incomprehension. Common meaning is actual in as much as there are common judgments, areas in which all affirm or deny in the same manner; and one withdraws from that common judgment when one disagrees. ... Common meaning is realized by decisions and choices, especially by permanent dedication, in the love that makes families, in the loyalty that makes states, in the faith that makes religion (Lonergan 1972:79).

What follows from this line of thought is decisive for the relationship between the culture, through which a people learns to be human, and the religious component of that culture. Their human community, and in some measure the integral humanness of each person, "coheres or divides, begins or ends, just where the common field of experience, common understanding, common judgment, common commitments begin and end" (ibid.). A culturally integrated religion can communicate meaningful answers to questions about the vast unknown. It helps to maintain unity among contemporaries of the same culture group, as well as continuity between their past and future generations. It also lends coherence to all the other elements of the culture upon which the people's plausible order of existence depends and without which social chaos inevitably breaks in and takes over.

We depend upon symbol systems to provide plausible, if not fully comprehensible, meanings for the mysteries of life. An example would be the Judeo-Christian idea of divine providence. God takes his own people by the hand as they walk through the precarious valley of shadows: "God is light" (1 Jn 1:5); his word enlightens everyone (cf. Jn 1:9; 8:12). The Hindu idea of reincarnation as a way of addressing the anxieties associated with a merely common-sense perception of human finitude is another example. A Sanskrit phrase of three words *tat tvam asi* ("that thou art") is perhaps the most important religious symbol in India for the rich and multiple meanings it conveys to devout Hindus (cf. Smith 1972:31).

Religions appeal to people because they offer plausible ways of coping not only with natural anxieties and mundane miseries but also and especially with uncanny forces and mysterious powers, and also with the inexplicable longings and aspirations of the human heart. The symbols of these religions, fragile webs that they are, offer the signs of hope and liberation that every human being needs. Religions also help to prevent terror and confusion from breaking in upon people when, confronted with a "tumult of uninterpretable events," they have reached the limits of their analytic capacities and moral insights (Geertz 1973:89). Then they cry out, or perhaps whisper, "my God" (*mein Gott, mon Dieu, Enkai ai*)! Even the flickering flame of a candle or a dark cloud in the sky may convey a hopeful reply.

A culture is a complex of such symbol systems, including with language and religion such things as law, ethics, aesthetics, education, science (mythology, philosophy, theology), entertainment, governance, marriage, child rearing, inheritance, security, economics and everything else people must learn in order to survive humanly. As a complex of symbol systems a culture embodies, codifies, integrates and communicates humanly constructed and historically transmitted patterns of meaning, perceptions, values, ideas, attitudes, judgments, beliefs, ideals, aspirations, commitments and actions through which life is interpreted more or less coherently and structured more or less consistently, at least plausibly, in accord with its own supportive ethos and world view (cf. Geertz 1973:89–90).

When a missionary from an alien cultural world either ignores or attacks any of the central cultural achievements (for example, language, law, religion, ethics, art) of the people to whom he or she has been sent, a process of cultural disintegration is fostered. The decline is hastened by increased zeal in replacing indigenous cultural elements and systems with foreign imports. The progressive elimination of a key component like religion amounts to a mutilation of a people's integrated sociocultural complex. An unbalanced ethos and world view is inevitable as efforts to compensate lead only to further distortions followed by an eventual tearing apart of the body social. Convenient theories may be called upon to "justify" this calculated mischief. For, as Bernard Lonergan notes, the process is "screened by self-deception," so the dissolution of a culture may even be "admired as the forward march of progress," while the evident ills brought forth are thought to be "remedied, not by a return to the misguided past, but by more elimination, mutilation, distortion"—until, in the end, the people's "cultural soul has been rendered incapable of reasonable convictions and responsible commitments" (Lonergan 1972:244).

VARIABILITY AND DIVERSITY OF SYMBOL SYSTEMS

Basically cultures are made and continuously reshaped by the human creativity of groups responding to the demands of the bio-climatic regions and historical periods in which they happen to find themselves seeking a livelihood with a measure of security and dignity. Of necessity the cultures of desert inhabitants must be vastly different from the ways of people living in the arctic tundra, by the sea, in fertile valleys, on mountain slopes, or in centers of commerce. For this reason cultures are not comparable in terms of better or worse, higher or lower. Each culture is a unique contribution to the human enterprise, a manifestation of the freedom and flexibility of human creativity. Each is an educational and humanizing memorial to the creative genius of our species.

At the same time, like everything human, cultures are all susceptible to corruption; hence they are always in need of reformation from within. The degeneration of German culture during the period of Hitler's National Socialism is a case in point. The corruption is not intrinsic to, nor typical of, the culture as such. It is not that some cultures are good and others evil. All may be regarded as good, although always in need of liberation from the evil inclinations perennially plaguing the human sojourn.

Like the sounds used by a language to communicate meanings to those understanding the language, religious symbols (for example, a cross for Christians, a *sathio* for Jains, a crescent for Muslims, a circle for Oglala Sioux) store and convey meanings by making tangible in the symbol a notion abstracted and recalled from past experience. A system of such symbols, embodying ideas, attitudes, values, judgments, longings, ideals, models and beliefs, speaks mightily to the followers of that religion as it makes present the experience, thereby awakening a variety of associated feelings and opening up new vistas capable of transforming human consciousness. Such transformations, as we know from history, sometimes act like the sound of trumpets setting armies in motion. Religions, again like languages, are essentially social constructions intimately connected with the other elements making up the whole culture of a people. Religions are "as public as marriage and as observable as agriculture" (Geertz 1973:91), and they are no less pervasive.

In every culture group (ethnic community, people, nation, class) there are many, sometimes a majority, who do not learn their own language very well. So also with the local religion; it is taken seriously only in varying degrees by its own followers, some of whom may be quite impious or even atheistic. The same may be said of other elements in any culture: laws, morals, customs, aesthetics, and so on. Whole societies have been known to abandon their languages as well as their religions, substituting in their stead inventions borrowed from, or imposed by, alien groups—usually as a result of enslavement, colonialism or imperialism of one type or another.

RELIGION AND POLITICS

Whatever historical transitions or upheavals may occur, and in spite of long intervals of religious decadence or declining faith, a felt need for religion periodically asserts itself in each cultural world, variously expressing itself according to laws not of logic but of image and feeling. The catalytic force and mass appeal of religious symbols periodically astonish common-sense planners and confound pragmatic organizers working on the flat level of mere secularity. The political significance, or this-worldly power, of such symbols is manifest today, for example, through the ayatollahs in Iran, the black madonna of Czestochowa in Poland, and the Exodus theme of Latin American liberation theologies now stirring the hearts of disadvantaged and oppressed peoples in other parts of the world. "Religion," said George Bernard Shaw, "is a great force—the only real motive force in the world." This insight has not always been appreciated by politicians, much less by Christian missionaries for whom Shaw's next line is especially relevant: "What you fellows don't understand is that you must get at a man through his own religion and not through yours" (quoted in Fulbright 1966:18).

Religious themes, laws, customs and personalities sometimes come to dominate entire societies, producing theocratic forms of government. Such concentrations of power, whether in ancient Israel, in Islamic nations, or in former European unions of church and state, end up in the hands of elite groups who too easily exploit religious symbols as means of pursuing their mundane goals. Ayatollahs, like some former popes, are thus empowered to send thousands of chanting young people to futile deaths in wars decreed holy by a clique of politicians in religious garb.

Because of the potential political power of religion, empire builders, when they cannot co-opt, control or moderate the religions of their subjects, try to destroy them or to manufacture substitutes that deify the empire or the emperor (liberator, chairman, leader, *Füher*, *duce*). In the past, for example, there was the Greco-Roman liturgy of the divine Caesars. In our time there are the Soviet rituals of Marxist-Leninism. A milder form of deified imperialism is reflected in a brand of American civil religion marked by pious political rhetoric and inflated nationalism often associated with military parades, competitive capitalism and football games.

BEYOND THE EPHEMERAL

Neither common sense nor scientific thinking suffices to reveal the meaning of the perplexity, pain, tragedy and moral paradox pervading human life, much less the meaning of life itself and the cold definitiveness of death. Pragmatic manipulators of power and their social engineers, functioning empirically on the level of naive common sense, deny by their deeds the meanings they proclaim in their political prattle about progress, freedom and security. Artists and poets come closer to reality with their poignant descriptions, but the full meaning eludes them. The hopeful disclosures sometimes offered in their exquisite articulations are too fragile and fleeting. It is from the perspective of the religious believer that the "really real," beyond all ephemeral appearances, is penetrated and the authentic meaning of events disclosed through symbols capable of putting to rest, by transcending them, the varied anxieties of the human heart.

"By entering the ritual," David Tracy tells us, "by retelling the myth, even by creatively reinterpreting the symbol, we escape from the 'nightmare' of history and even the 'terror' of ordinary time." Through religious symbols, myths and rituals that use ordinary media (rocks, water, fire, mountains, clouds) people can reach the "other side of the ordinary" and become "saturated with a power that is *sheerly* given—but given only in the manifestation, the hierophanies and theophonies of the sacred" (Tracy 1981:205–6). Religious ritual enactments thus contribute to the transformation of consciousness through which the ontologically real, as distinguished from merely palpable reality, may be glimpsed by mortal eyes.

The Maasai people of Kenya and Tanzania have a traditional story— which is substantially identical with a myth handed down among the Dinka people of southern Sudan—to cope with, by explaining the meaning of, the bafflement, pain and moral paradox felt by everyone.[1] It is the story of an original fault committed by some people but affecting the destinies of all in relation to one another and to the God of all. Belief in a beneficent divinity, an original harmony and human solidarity, is presupposed and beyond question in these preliterate societies of sub-Saharan Africa. In spite of all the perplexing, painful, paradoxical and tragic events characterizing the human condition, a dramatic story expresses and affirms a hopeful belief that things really are under control and in order, and that there is a believable explanation, a humanly intelligible story, that makes sense and provides the meaning of it all.

Because of an original offense, the divinity is no longer close and familiar but withdrawn and yet present in mysterious ways indicated through symbols. Supreme magnanimity for the Maasai people is symbolized by the dark clouds that bring rain, hence life; omnipotence is symbolized by the full sky designated by the same word used for the deity, *enkai*, with the diminutive/feminine prefix *en* connoting reverence. It is hard to imagine a more appropriate symbol for that ultimate horizon of hope which Jews and Christians haltingly name *Yahweh* or *Elohim* or God: the ineffable, indefinable, absolute, infinite, incomprehensible, unfathomable mystery and ground of all reality and of every particular existent (cf. Rahner *FC* 1978:chap. 2).

DOING WHAT IS SIGNIFIED

For those who have learned to believe, religious symbols make unfathomable mysteries plausible, incomprehensible events explicable, a sense of justice tangible, human life endurable and the future hopeful. Christians cope with the mystery of evil and death through the symbol of the risen Christ. This symbol is at once a pledge of humankind's victory over evil, which, on account of Adam's sin, is present actively and passively in the lives of all the children of Adam. On account of the Second Adam, however, liberation from enslavement to sin with its sinister consequences is possible for all (cf. Rom 5). In both instances the deliberate act of one human being standing symbolically for all (corporate personality) embraces the whole of humankind, recalling the solidarity lost through sin yet available through faith in the promises, the "good news" of the one who, in the long run, is victorious by being the person for others.

Faith in the veracity and reliability of the available religious symbol system is tangibly and often powerfully reinforced, if not in some measure also generated, by rituals. Recall the moods and motivations sometimes generated in ourselves by funeral rites, even when we may not have known personally the deceased. A liturgical presentation of the Jewish Passover story can also be profoundly moving even for persons who may not share the faith of Israel. The very impressive fertility rites of Maasai women are capable of inspiring confidence, renewing faith and generating hope not only among the Maasai but also among people from different cultural worlds and with different religious backgrounds.

In this sense religious faith can awaken in people as they portray it in drama or rituals. As Christian theologians say of the sacraments: they do what they signify; or, what they celebrate becomes present through them. At the very least, even an outside observer is apt to feel that the fertility chants of Maasai women, as they process confidently around a massive tree in the forest while offering (just as their mothers and grandmothers did before them under the same tree) libations of fresh cows' milk sprinkled on the ancient tree trunk with an aspergillum made from a clump of green grass, must certainly be heard above the clouds. The actual participants in the ritual, all in garb signifying a state of liminality, far from having any doubts at all, are confident of having healthy children born to them within a reasonable time. A deep sense of trust and hope becomes palpable through the ritual. Such moods and motivations induce in people what Clifford Geertz calls a "general conception of the order of existence" more firmly established in reality than any conception of order resting merely on an empirically scientific "swirl of probabilistic hypotheses" (Geertz 1973:112).

Geertz continues, "Whatever role divine intervention may or may not play in the creation of faith, . . . it is, primarily at least, out of the context of concrete acts of religious observance that religious convictions emerge on the human plane" (ibid.). It is not, of course, a few ritual enactments alone that produce faith in a particular conceptualization of a plausible order of existence; it is, rather, a large and public complex of varied symbol systems interacting as a generally integrated cultural performance, celebrating the meaning of reality and thereby shaping the consciousness, understanding and outlook of a whole people. A Zoroastrian wedding celebration might be taken as an example of a ritual enactment that signifies and renews a community's integrated cultural ethos and world view more realistically than all the careful calculations of Zoroastrian shopkeepers.

DEFINING RELIGION

So it is that people need their religions as much as their languages. Religious symbol systems are capable of communicating to them the meaning of the "really real" in their cultural worlds; and it is meaning that holds things together even on the brink of chaos. Religions, at their best, can do this, as Geertz suggests in his detailed anthropological analysis of religious phenomena. As defined by Geertz, religion is "a system of symbols which acts to establish powerful, pervasive, and long-lasting moods and motivations . . . by formulating conceptions of a general order of existence and clothing these conceptions with such an aura of factuality that the moods and the motivations seem uniquely realistic" (Geertz 1973:90).

For George Santayana the great power of a religion "consists in its special and surprising message and in the bias which that revelation gives to life. The vistas it opens and the mysteries it propounds are another world to live in, and another world to live in — whether we expect ever to pass wholly over into it or no — is what we mean by having a religion" (quoted in Geertz 1973:87). A similar but broader definition is offered by Hans Küng:

Religion is a *believing view of life, approach to life, way of life*, and therefore a *fundamental pattern* embracing the individual and society, man and the world, through which a person (though only partially conscious of this) sees and experiences, thinks and feels, acts and suffers, everything. It is a transcendentally grounded and immanently operative *system of coordinates*, by which man orients himself intellectually, emotionally, and existentially (Küng 1986:xvi).

According to this definition, which seems to include the previous ones, "religion provides a comprehensive meaning for life, guarantees supreme values and unconditional norms, creates a spiritual community and home" (ibid.).

CORRUPTIBILITY

Like all the products of human creativity the components of any culture, as indeed whole cultures themselves, are susceptible to distortion and corruption. The constructions of theologians, when they become petrified beliefs, can be just as dangerous to people as the theories of politicians, economists and generals. The danger is acute when priests, rabbis, imams, pastors, prelates, gurus or shamans bless these theoretical constructs and sacralize them with the symbols of religion. In European history this is exemplified by the mutual slaughter of Christians in their numerous "holy wars" against each other in the name of the same God whom they reduced to a manageable mundane level and split into local gods. The "holy" Inquisitions of Spain and of Rome, vigorously promoted by church leaders with no qualms about the torture and extermination of persons whose thinking was persistently "incorrect," are also well-known examples of religion's gory deviations in behalf of theoretical purity. It suffices here to recall Pope Leo X, who declared against Martin Luther, the challenger of Leo's fundraising methods, that "the burning of heretics is fully in accord with the will of the Holy Spirit" (quoted in Rahner *TI* 14:96).

During most of the history of Christianity, moreover, church leaders, theologians, canonists, exegetes and living saints saw no incompatibility between the central message of Jesus and the socioeconomic institution of slavery. St. Augustine considered slavery a punishment for sin. St. Thomas Aquinas integrated the punishment-for-sin theory into his natural law ethics where slavery was considered as inevitable as growing old, regrettable but in accord with the natural law (*ST* Suppl., q 52, a 1, ad 2 & 3; a 3, respon.; Ia-IIae, q 94, a 5, ad 3; IIa-IIae, q 57, a 3, ad 2).

In the period just before the American Civil War, Bishop John England of Charleston, on behalf of the Catholic Bishops of the United States, presented to the American Secretary of State, John Forsyth, an elaborate defense of domestic slavery. The bishops argued thus:

Slavery . . . is regarded by the church of which the pope is the presiding officer not to be incompatible with the natural law, to be the result of sin by divine dispensation, to have been established by human legislation, and when the dominion of the slave has been justly acquired by the master to be lawful, not only in the sight of the human tribunal but also in the eyes of Heaven (England 5 1908:195).

Even after the fratricidal war between the States, when slavery had already been abolished in most countries by the secular authorities, the *Inquisitores Generales* of the Holy Office in Rome (formerly the Inquisition, now the Congregation for the Doctrine of the Faith) still taught that, "according to the approved theologians and interpreters of the sacred canons," it is "not contrary to natural and divine law for slaves to be sold, bought, exchanged or given." So, "Christians may lawfully buy slaves and accept them in payment of a debt or as a gift" (*Propaganda Fidei* 1, 1907:719).

Such thinking flows logically from the "classicist mentality," described already, which categorized slaves simply as property. In this view it would be morally wrong to buy or accept slaves "who had been stolen from their lawful owner," as the *inquisitores* said, because "it is wrong to buy property taken by theft" (ibid.). Fortunately a contrary opinion was promoted persistently by some non-approved "theologians and interpreters of the sacred canons."

Perhaps the most shocking instance of religion's corruptibility in the Western hemisphere is the bloody worship offered to the Aztec god Quetzalcoatl atop the great pyramid of Cholula in Tenochtitlan (now Mexico City) where it is estimated that thousands of human victims were sacrificed annually (cf. Berger 1974:93). In the same place this murderous form of worship was later emulated by Hernando Cortes and other conquistadors in behalf of their Spanish colonial gods of gold and power.

History is replete with adequate evidence to support a widespread belief in humankind's fallen condition. Martin Luther's *"ecclesia semper reformanda"* dictum is lapidary. Not only the church but all religions, marked as they are by human stupidity, greed, vanity, pride, cruelty, arrogance, frailty and shame, are "always in need of reform." The cleansing of the temple by reform or renewal, after careful critical research, is a perennial task for people who take religion seriously not for what they can get out of it for themselves, but for what it is in itself.

GUIDELINES FOR JUDGING RELIGIONS

If religions, like their human creators, are both corruptible and correctable, then assessments must be made about what in them is so deviant that reform is needed. What moral parameters do we have for making judgments about the strengths and weaknesses, the good and bad, the right and wrong, in any religion?

Relevant indicators, with common characteristics reflecting a concern for the same values and suggesting the existence of universal human norms, may be found in various religions. The unity of love of God and love of neighbor as a criterion for authentic Christian behavior is not far from the Confucian ideal of *jen*, which means loving others joyously and with one's whole heart. Nor is the Confucian concept of *shu* other than the Golden Rule of Christians or the *Mahabharata* of Hinduism (cf. Bluhm 1984:296–97). Buddhists put it thus: "As a mother even at the risk of her own life watches over her own child, so let everyone cultivate a boundless love toward all beings" (quoted in Maguire 1979:76). These and similar imperatives found in other religions, and their corollaries concerned with equity, would seem to warrant the following guidelines.

First, as a cultural institution intended to serve universal human values by responding to real needs experienced by people in their respective sociocultural and historical situations, it might be said that a given religion is true or worthy or authentic insofar as it helps to give its followers an awareness of what is truly ultimate and most meaningful. In the search for ultimately meaningful reality, the "really real," people usually follow paths already opened for them by their progenitors, whether these ways lead inwardly toward the psychic depths of humankind or outwardly toward a totally other power or source, or incomprehensible ground of all reality, whether left unnamed or called God, gods or spirits.

A second criterion might be the question whether and to what extent this religion assists its faithful adherents in loving other human beings as they love themselves—with a love that is founded on respect for human dignity and justice, understood as fairness in the distribution of the benefits and burdens of life.

A third criterion might be a religion's ability to lead people beyond themselves to new levels of consciousness, freedom, openness, hope and confidence in an ultimate order of meaningful existence.

While these guidelines are interrelated and involve transcendence, each has a particular focus. The first concerns especially the unknown other, usually labelled God or gods or spirits. The second looks to relations among members of the human family: the common good or general welfare of all. The third concerns transcendence specifically.

RELIGION AND ETHICS

Ethics is understood here as a systematic set of norms and rules for the guidance of human conduct in the moral domain, that is, in reference to what is considered right or wrong, good or bad, virtue or vice, value or disvalue. Such systems, like languages and religions, are found in all cultures. Often the connection between ethics and religion is so intimate that religious faith is assumed to be the inspiration, if not the source, of morally upright behavior. The apparent dependence of ethics upon religion is further confirmed by the moral sensitivity generally reflected in religious teachings. Religious teachers and prophets never tire of reminding their hearers of the ominous moral consequences of any decline in religious practices.

The assumption that ethics depends on religion becomes dubious, however, when it is noticed that sometimes high levels of moral decency are reflected consistently in the lives of persons who are explicitly irreligious or even atheistic. The assumption is more questionable still in the light of what is known about the horrendous injustices officially perpetrated or tolerated over the ages in the name of religion, for example, the torture and murder of masses of alleged heretics and witches, or the enslavement of some people for the enrichment of others.

Although some religions (for example, Islam) seem to have developed their own ethical systems, it can be argued persuasively, at least within the terms of the Christian tradition, that dependence upon organized religion is not intrinsic to the nature of morality, which is much broader than the selected ethical norms and orientations emphasized variously in religious teachings. Citing Thomas Aquinas in support of this position, Edward Schillebeeckx asserts that "the specific character of the ethics of Christians . . . lies in the fact that it has no ethics of its own and is therefore open to the *humanum* which is sought by all men and women, here and now and ever anew" (1987:50). Indeed, the ethics of Western Christians owe more to Aristotelianism and to Stoicism than to the books of the Bible. Rational reflection upon human experience has been more relied upon than revelation for the formulation of ethical norms and rules for differentiating right from wrong. Even the ethical teachings attributed to Jesus by the New Testament authors did not originate with him; they were already present within the cultural ethos of his time and place. His sources were developed through the human experience of his own people and handed down from generation to generation in their cultural world which, in turn, borrowed from the moral wisdom of other peoples more ancient than themselves as well as from the cultures of their contemporaries.

The first Christians could no more have invented a new ethical system than they could a new language. According to biblical scholar J. L. Houlden, St. Paul certainly appears to have assumed as his own Christian ethical scheme the contemporary "ethical ideals and concepts of pagan society." This is "explicit in his remarks about the universal moral consciousness of man (Rom 2:14)," says Professor Houlden, "and implicit in his straightforward and almost unmodified adoption of conventional pagan lists of virtues and vices, of the terms of current (especially Stoic) ethics, and of catalogues of household duties . . . simply accepting these elements as parts of the common air which all men breathe" (Houlden 1973:93).[2]

The point to be made is that any ethical system, however intimately associated with religion, rests at bottom upon a secular foundation of common human experience. With or without the help of religion generations of people work out and hand on systems for dealing with universally experienced human situations involving truth-telling, respect for life, the distribution of resources, fairness in dealing with others, the responsible exercise of freedom, man-woman relations, child-rearing, adjudication, security, social participation, modes of governance, and so forth. While religions are certainly concerned with such matters, they are nevertheless pre-religious secular realities that all cultures deal with through their respective ethical systems, which are cultural components analogous to languages. The moral sensitivity and wisdom derived from generations of common human experience is irreducible. These are not created by religions, much less are they generated by theological conceptualizations or imagery, although these can be, and usually are, valuable supports for ethical systems.

THE SAME BUT DIFFERENT

Religions have common purposes insofar as they meet the same general needs experienced by all human beings and find a place in all cultures, but they are not all just the same. "No two religious traditions are alike just as no two individuals are alike," says Burlan A. Sizemore, Jr., "but it remains true that in terms of religious phenomenology the Christian experience is not radically different from others" (Sizemore 1976:416). Indeed, all religious experience, aside from its myriad historico-cultural particularizations, consists at bottom in the experience of God, the experience of self and the encounter with our neighbor, for we experience ourselves by experiencing other persons, not other things. "All these three experiences," in the words of Karl Rahner, "ultimately constitute a single reality with three aspects mutually conditioning one another" (*TI* 13:128).

Again, religions resemble languages, which serve the same general purposes but with varied emphases, forms, symbols, styles and organizational schemes. We do not say that French is a better language than English. Yet we recognize that some thoughts can hardly be expressed as well in one of these languages as in the other. This is why languages borrow from one another.

We know also that most people cannot achieve in a foreign language the same facility they have in their native tongue. Each religion, like each language, and every other cultural creation, has its peculiar strengths and weaknesses. So as outside observers we do not say that Islam is a better religion than Hinduism. Each in its own way is a more appropriate symbol system, just as a particular language is, for the people who were socialized into it, and into no other.

A people's faith in an established order of existence that accords with their ethos and world view, as already suggested, occurs within and is expressed through and sustained by an integrated complex of symbol systems, that is, their particular culture. The religious component of the culture, while in a dynamic relationship of mutual dependence and interaction with the other systems in the same complex, is particularly concerned with the search for, and expression of, meaning in the face of the vast unknown. So the genesis, expression and maintenance of faith is appropriately and commonly attributed to the religious system.

The faith proffered to every person, which each is free to reject, is normally expressed through the material of his or her religious tradition (beliefs, rites, customs, and so on) handed down from those whose generations of experience provided the vantage point and focus of that faith. The faith of Christians, for example, has historical continuity and cultural affinity not only with the faith of Jesus and the apostles but also with the faith of Israel extending back to Abraham. Through the faith of Abraham, and the wider ecumenical vision of Christians today, common ground with the faith of Islam is also recognized (*NA* 3; cf. Küng 1986:122–26). There are, moreover, increasing efforts to explore and explicate the implicit commonalities of all religious systems.

A recognition of the validity of each religion for its own adherents does not imply that all faith communities are equal in every way, or that each has nothing to learn from the varied historico-cultural ways in which faith is expressed in different religious systems, or even in the same religion under the influence of diverse cultures and historical periods. As Paul Knitter points out in his carefully nuanced discussion of this point, particular beliefs held in one faith community may offer a more adequate and credible image of the deity than certain beliefs associated with another religion. "Of two religious attitudes," says Knitter, "one advocating the burning of widows, and the other the equality of all men and women, most persons would venture the judgment that one is a more adequate and relevant articulation of religious experience than the other" (Knitter 1985:52). And what is to be said of a religious attitude that righteously insists on straining out every gnat of deviant sexual behavior while showing little indignation over the causes of world hunger or the in-place plans for the massive thermonuclear extermination of humankind?

So differences do matter, even to the extent of suggesting that, in a number of important ways, one religion might be said to express its faith more adequately than another. At least this suggests that, through dialogue with the followers of other religions, one faith community might be led to reexamine some of its beliefs and to modify some of its practices, thereby improving its own expressions of faith.

COMMON GROUND OF FAITH

Insofar as the cumulative religious tradition of a people is the mundane result of their faith in the past and the mundane source of that people's faith today, as Wilfred Cantwell Smith argues, every religiously conscious person or community is the locus of a transaction between the transcendent, which is presumably the same for every person, and the cumulative tradition, which is different for each people, nation or ethnic-culture group (cf.

Smith 1978:186). Belief (with everything else that constitutes a particular religious system) is thus distinguishable from faith. Between the two there is a dynamic relationship of mutual interaction. This is analogous to the relationship between language and understanding; each operates only through the other.

As David Tracy says, there is "no purely nonlinguistic 'understanding' " (1981:101). Nor is there a pure faith that remains without a symbol system, usually religious, as its means of expression. As conceptualization and understanding presuppose the existence of a language for the articulation of thoughts, so faith needs a belief system for its manifestation. "From the beginning to the end of our journey to understand," Tracy continues, "we find ourselves in a particular linguistic tradition (primarily our native language) which carries with it a certain specifiable way of viewing the world, certain 'forms of life' which we did not invent but find ourselves within" (ibid.).

Understanding, as an event of human experience within a particular historico-cultural context, is mediated through, hence shaped and influenced by, the past experience and understanding embodied in each particular linguistic tradition. Analogously, faith is mediated through the inherited belief system of a people. As a language presupposes and serves the common human capacity for understanding, so belief presupposes and serves the common human capacity for faith. But this is more than a matter of capacity. In terms of actual human existence in the particularity of history and culture, a people's understanding depends necessarily upon the linguistic system concretely available to them, usually their native language. Likewise, a people's faith depends necessarily upon the belief system concretely available to them, usually their particular religious heritage. Faith and belief are thus inseparable but distinguishable. With due attention to Knitter's cautionary remarks, noted in the previous section, this distinction may be accepted as "valid," "indispensable" and "necessary" (Knitter 1985:51).

Christian tradition provides grounds for believing that faith is gratuitously proffered by God to every human being, because God truly wills the salvation of everyone. This faith, at bottom, consists in our radical and free acceptance (or non-rejection) of the rational and historico-cultural human nature that, while defining us, enables us to become what we are supposed to be in relation to God and to one another.[3] To this basic notion of faith, "even in the strictly Christian meaning of the term," must be added Karl Rahner's provision "that this faith should really be understood as being sustained and empowered by the transcendent nature of this very rationality, in which the latter is merged into the incomprehensible mystery we call 'God' with which we inevitably have to do in this experience of our transcendental nature, whether we consciously define that nature or not" (*TI* 17:64).

If Jews, Muslims and Christians, in spite of differences in their respective beliefs, share a common faith with Abraham (and even some common beliefs), then further study, dialogue and reflection may reveal wider commonalities also with the followers of all the other belief systems. "By distinguishing belief and faith," says Bernard Lonergan, "we have secured a basis both for ecumenical encounter and for an encounter between all religions with a basis in religious experience." While religions may differ greatly, there is behind them a commonality of faith providing "a deeper unity." In Lonergan's view, like that of Wilfred Cantwell Smith, "beliefs result from judgments of value, and judgments of value relevant to religion come from faith" (Lonergan 1972:118–19;122–24; cf. also Panikkar 1979: chap. 6; Lane 1981: chap 3; Rahner *SM* 2:311–12).[4]

2

Christian Theology and the Ubiquity of Grace

Faith, as indicated in the foregoing pages, is the most basic and dynamic feature that all viable religious systems are apt to have in common. For this reason the religions of the world may be understood as communities of faith, however much they may differ in their respective beliefs and practices. What have Christian theologians to say about the salutary significance of these religious communities? Before answering this question we should first examine what the theologians have been saying up to now concerning the nature and availability of grace for the salvation of humankind—salvation being understood generally to mean "the strictly supernatural and divine presence of God in himself," afforded as unmerited grace, proffered as divine life and friendship, made manifest in an orientation of life marked by faith, hope and love (cf. Rahner *TI* 16:56–57, 200).

Our understanding of intellection shapes our appreciation of humankind's rich linguistic pluralism. In a similar manner our understanding of grace determines our perception of humankind's vast array of faith communities. What is said about grace in this chapter is, therefore, foundational for the reflections offered in the third chapter where the elements of a Christian theological interpretation of the world's abundant religious pluralism are set forth.

THEOLOGY AND BELIEF

Theology for Christians consists in conscious and methodical efforts to understand, explicate and explain not only the meaning of their faith but the truthfulness of it, as expressed in biblical revelation and in the beliefs developed and articulated by interpreters during the long course of Judeo-Christian history. As a human enterprise this theology has had, and continues to have, its low as well as its high periods of achievement.

Because theologians necessarily work only from the narrow vantage points available to them in their limited cultural worlds and brief historical moments, a measure of misunderstanding and confusion is inevitably found in, or attributed to, their writings when scrutinized by their students or examined critically by the inquisitors, grand and less than grand, of ecclesiastical officialdom. These scrutinies have sometimes led to the repudiation of theological positions once taken as official church teaching, and to the downgrading of the theologians once regarded as champions of orthodoxy. There is, for example, a long list of "approved theologians" who once maintained the compatibility of Christianity with the pernicious institution of slavery. Yesterday's orthodoxy sometimes becomes today's heterodoxy. The opposite also happens.

It is not only the opinions of theologians and responses of the Vatican congregations but also conciliar statements and pontifical pronouncements that have sometimes been subject to revision. If some of these teachings have been reinterpreted, reformulated or even contradicted in the past, then such revisions may also be appropriate in the future. Even the formally promulgated doctrines of the church under the mantle of infallibility are always presented in the garb of particular times and specific cultures. These formulations of belief are more like theological milestones than ultimate terminals of revealed truth. Indeed, it is appropriate to the nature of a pilgrim people that the truth should be understood only in progressive stages (cf. Fries, *SM* 3:137).

Historical change and cultural pluralism, however reluctantly acknowledged by the "classicist mentality," are characteristics intrinsic to the human enterprise. For this reason the shepherds of the Christian flocks have periodically tried to clarify and systematize the beliefs of Christians by formulating them abstractly as sets of propositions in fixed logical categories assumed to be timelessly universal. The belief system of Christians in the Catholic tradition is thus found not only in the Bible and in the works of the Church Fathers and later theologians but also in official dogmas, liturgies, doctrines, decrees, declarations, directives, constitutions, encyclicals, instructions, exhortations, admonitions, prohibitions, suspensions, interdictions and excommunications. Now that most countries prohibit the physical elimination of persons whose thinking is officially judged as incorrect, beliefs are also expressed by the "de-Catholicization" of dissenting theologians and by the humiliation of bishops who raise "untimely" questions concerning the pastoral implications of certain positions preferred by the church's servants at the higher levels of officialdom.

Since the shepherds have perennially shown themselves to be no less human than the theologians, it was found by later theologians, who convinced later shepherds, that the doctrinal formulations of the past needed to be interpreted critically just as all historically and culturally conditioned documents must be, including the Bible. Otherwise the authors' intended meanings cannot be understood properly and related faithfully to the hearers of their words in the contemporary world. As the decades pass, unprecedented experiences bring fresh insights, old words acquire different shades of meaning, novel perceptions result from varied vantage points, philosophical presuppositions are superseded, and ideological frames of reference are altered by additional information and broadened horizons. Without a rationally critical hermeneutic, moreover, a number of serious errors might have remained in the official belief system of the Christian community.

This problem may be illustrated by any number of historical examples. The nineteenth-century teaching of the Holy Office on slavery has already been noted in the previous chapter. The opinion of St. Augustine on the sin associated with marital copulation, repeated throughout the centuries in the formal teachings of bishops and popes (for example, Gregory the Great and Innocent III), was officially corrected only in the present century by Pope Pius XII (cf. Hillman 1975:25–27). And, of course, the Second Vatican Council reversed some long-standing teachings, such as the official position of the church on religious liberty (cf. O'Callaghan 1968:322; Schüller 1968:332; Burghardt 1968:310–15).

Far from weakening the faith of Christians or undermining their beliefs and practices, it is now widely recognized that the raising of critical questions can, in the words of Vatican II, "stimulate the mind to a more accurate and penetrating grasp of the faith" (*GS* 62), and this, after all, is what theology is all about. It is not only appropriate but necessary to raise questions that require new theological investigations in all areas of sociocultural importance, bringing to bear "a fresh scrutiny on the deeds and words which God has made known, which have been consigned to sacred Scripture, and which have been unfolded by the Church fathers and the teaching authority of the Church" (*AG* 22).

More than just an intellectual exercise for theologians, the Council envisages an opening for "a more profound adaptation of the whole area of Christian life," not only in the outward practices of religion and ecclesiastical organization, but also in the realm of "morality and doctrine" (*GS* 62). Even in this realm the pilgrim church is summoned "to that continual reformation of which she always has need, insofar as she is an institution of men here on earth" (*UR* 6). While this is said in the conciliar decree on ecumenism among separated Christian communities, it is also relevant to the wider ecumenism among the world's religions: "If the influence of events or the times had led to deficiencies in conduct, in Church discipline, or even in the formulation of doctrine (which must be carefully distinguished from the deposit of faith), these should be appropriately rectified at the proper moment" (ibid.).

This point about official changes in the belief system is germane to the far-reaching innovations implied in the Second Vatican Council's unexpected departure from the long-standing negative position of the official church regarding the other religions of the world. As a prelude to the questions raised by the church's new attitude toward these faith communities, the present chapter traces the historical changes in the theological understanding of the nature and the availability of God's saving grace.

OPTIMISM CONCERNING SALVATION

An early and constant tradition associated with the *Logos* theology of the Alexandria school, authoritatively rooted in the first chapter of the Fourth Gospel and reflected in a variety of other New Testament passages (for example, Mt 8:10; 25:31–46; Acts 10:34–35, 11:17–18; Rom 2:10–11, 5:12–21, 11:32; Heb 9:26–28; 2 Cor 5:15; 1 Tm 2:4; 1 Jn 4:7, 16), was full of hope for the salvation of the "good pagan." This optimism concerning the universal availability and the superabounding nature of God's saving grace, inundating the lives of all human beings even outside the visible structures of the church, is clearly expressed by some of the most important Christian writers of the first three centuries, for example, Clement of Rome (the third pope), Justin Martyr, Clement of Alexandria and Iranaeus. The following words of Justin (c. 100–165) are typical and might be taken as the primordial statement of Karl Rahner's modern theory of the "anonymous Christian."

We have been taught, are convinced and do believe, that God approves of only those who imitate his inherent virtues, namely, temperance, justice, love of humankind, and any other virtue proper to God who is called by no given name. If people by their actions prove themselves worthy of his plan, they shall be . . . found worthy to make their abode with him. . . . To do what pleases God, and to choose to do so through the intelligence he has given us . . . leads to faith.

We have been taught that Christ was the first begotten of God, and . . . the Word of whom all mankind partakes. Those who lived by reason are Christians, even though they have been considered atheists: such as, among the Greeks, Socrates, Heraclitus and others like them (*First Apology*, chaps. 10, 14).

There were, after all, according to the Bible, holy people who were neither Jews nor Christians, such as Noah, Melchisedech and Job. The biblical recognition of their holiness, which must be due to the grace of Christ as the unique savior of humankind, would seem to have implications for all who lived and died without any access to the biblical religions of Judaism and Christianity. It had to be appreciated by theologians, as Jean Danielou says in his study of the "holy pagans," that the righteous or just person is not one who conforms his or her conduct to what is right and true but one "whom God recognizes as righteous" (Danielou 1957:30).

The faith, without which it is impossible to please God, is found outside as well as inside the Judeo-Christian covenants (cf. Heb 11). Moreover, the

Spirit is like the wind, blowing wherever it pleases (Jn 3:8), and God enlightens everyone who comes into the world, bestowing them with "grace upon grace" (Jn 1:9–16), because he loves them all and truly wants each to be saved (1 Tm 2:4). In their respective cultural worlds, as St. Paul observed in Athens, people everywhere are "very religious" and God is not far from anyone, because all are "indeed his offspring" (Acts 17:22–28).

It was possible, therefore, to believe that such manifestly noble and wise individuals as Plato and Aristotle were responsive to the divine Logos universally present to humankind both before and after the advent of that same Word in the flesh of Jesus Christ. St. Iranaeus at the end of the second century taught that the divine Logos "was ever present to the human race until the day when he united himself with his creation and was made flesh" (*Adversus haereses* 3:6, 12–13, 16, 24; also 1: 3, 10; 4: 5–7, 20). St. Clement of Rome (pope from 88–97) put it thus: "From generation to generation the Lord has given opportunity of repentance to all who would turn to him." To illustrate the point, Clement refers to the salvation of all who responded to the preaching of Noah and of Jonah, "although they were aliens to God" (*Epist. 1 ad Cor.*, chap. 7).

Clement of Alexandria (150–215) is especially interesting on this point because of his explicit mention of different cultural worlds having their respective covenants: "All authentic understanding or wisdom is sent by God . . . and the true teacher of the Egyptians, the Indians, the Babylonians and the Persians, indeed of all created beings, is the first-begotten Son, the fellow counselor of God." According to Clement, "philosophy was given to the Greeks as a covenant peculiar to them; many are the different covenants of the Lord with humankind," because "the Lord is upon many waters (Ps 29:3), and his beneficence is not limited to particular places or persons" (*Stromata*, bk. 4, c.8).

These theologians were not blinded by their confidence in the ubiquity of the divine Logos. Their writings abound with severe criticisms of the religious cults of their own time. But these negative pronouncements, according to Henri de Lubac, must not be taken as universally normative value judgments on all non-Christian religions (1967:68–75). Even the optimistic statements cited above (and there are many more of them) should be seen against the firmly held patristic belief in the definitive action of the divine Logos in Jesus Christ

PESSIMISM CONCERNING SALVATION

The good news enunciated by the early apologists and theologians just cited was subsequently clouded over by the somber views of other theologians perhaps less able to transcend the Stoic and Manichaean gloom that permeated much of the Mediterranean cultural world. Social, economic and political factors were also at work as the numbers of Roman Christians increased, especially after the Edict of Milan in 313. During this period the question of religious pluralism was raised and debated.

Probably because he saw the handwriting on the wall, the Roman Senator Quintus Aurelius Symmachus, an apologist for the traditional culture-religions of the Greco-Roman world, declared it "impossible that so great a mystery should be approached by one road only" (quoted in Toynbee 1957:112–17; 1956:253, 279, 299). Symmachus was not converted to the beliefs of the new faith community by his protagonist, St. Ambrose of Milan. By the time of the Senator's death in 410, not only had Christianity become the official religion of the Roman Empire but all the other religions had been proscribed. Shortly thereafter non-Christians were even excluded from holding public office. An identification of the Christian faith community with the political, economic and security interests of the Roman Empire would doubtless have reinforced the exclusivistic tendencies already developed when, before Constantine, Christians were treated as outsiders and periodically persecuted by the religio-political establishment then in power.

In the theological tradition of Clement of Alexandria, the church was not seen merely as a historically tangible institution; it was also the community of all who responded to God's grace from the time of Abel, that is, all who are just in the sight of God. But when Cyprian (c. 210–258), borrowing an axiom from Clement's famous student Origen, spoke of "no salvation outside the church," he took it literally and gave it a juridically restrictive meaning in relation to the church as a historically established social institution.

St. Augustine, a former student of St. Ambrose, recognized the broad sense of the "church from the time of Abel," but he was ambivalent about its implications and leaned heavily toward the pessimistic understanding of salvation for those living beyond the juridical borders of explicit membership in the visible church. Karl Rahner attributes this to Augustine's insufficient attention to the pre-Nicene and Greek theology of grace. Augustine "understood too little of the earlier theology, that precisely the Logos is the one who appears and must appear if God wants to show himself personally to the world" (*NG*:24). Even infants dying without baptism were, according to Augustine, punished by eternal hellfire. In his critique Rahner asserts "that Augustine inaugurated and taught to Christendom a view of world-history according to which . . . world-history remained the history of the *massa damnata* from which in the last resort, by a rarely granted grace of election, only a few were saved" (*TI* 20:99–100). Because of his great prominence as a theologian, Augustine's grim opinions in this area gained general acceptance. Later historical events contributed further support to his pessimistic interpretation of God's justice.

THE RISE OF ISLAM

Negative attitudes toward "infidels" were fostered also by the later emergence of Islam as an alien religio-political system threatening the Christian hegemony in the Mediterranean world. The anxieties of Christians, who witnessed the growing vitality of Islam among the Arab peoples, may well have been the most significant factor contributing to a negative appreciation of the workings of grace outside the church. In less than one generation after the death of Muhammad (c. 632) Arab war lords were ruling in Syria, Palestine, Mesopotamia and Tripoli, with all of North Africa and parts of Europe on the verge of succumbing to an alien religio-political movement. Inevitably, following the lead of St. John of Damascus in the middle of the eighth century, Christian theologians denounced Islam as a heresy, thus reaffirming the doubts about the possibility of salvation for such people. It was not, however, until 1095 that the first of a long series of Crusades got underway, generating great animosity not only toward the followers of Islam but also, by implication, toward all the "infidels" of every "heathen" religion.

LIMBO AND BAPTISM OF DESIRE

The basic optimism of some of the earliest Christian writers concerning unbaptized persons was not totally smothered by the dire judgments of later theologians whose views, supported by ominous quotations from such notables as Augustine, Cyprian and Fulgentius of Ruspe, found their way into the official teachings of the church. Peter Abelard (1079–1142) wrestled with the theological issue, specifically in reference to Augustine's teaching on the fate of unbaptized infants. As an alternative, Abelard came up with a compromise theory borrowed from Pelagius that placed these infants neither in heaven nor in hell but somewhere in between, labelled "limbo" by Albertus Magnus. This was subsequently taken up by others as a way of explaining the plight not only of unbaptized infants but of all who, through no fault of their own, were untouched by the saving waters of baptism.

Because of the necessity of baptism for salvation and the fact that some people, through no fault of their own, had no access to this ritual enactment, some kind of implicit membership in the church was a rational postulate based on God's will that all should be saved (1 Tm 2:4). There had to be a kind of baptism of desire implying at least implicit faith and membership in the church. This theological notion was developed initially in reference to isolated pastoral cases within Christendom. What was the status of a person who, for some obscure reason, had not been baptized with water but had died after a lifetime of exemplary Christian living? An official basis for the idea of baptism of desire is found in a letter attributed to Pope Innocent III, referring to the teachings of Augustine and Ambrose regarding "baptism ministered invisibly" (Denzinger 1957, no.388). In another context, however, the same pope insisted upon the ancient axiom that "outside the holy Roman Catholic Church . . . no one is saved" (ibid. 423). This belief was echoed a few years later, only in a passing manner, by the Fourth Lateran Council (ibid. 430).

Toward the end of his life St. Thomas Aquinas (1225–74) probably considered the questions raised by the Polo expeditions, but he had already treated the salvation question in terms of a hypothetical case of an unbaptized child who, lost in a European forest, grew up invincibly ignorant of the gospel message. Citing an opinion of Augustine, Thomas argued that in some extraordinary cases salvation is possible without baptism of water, hence without juridical membership in the church. "Having weighed this again and again," says Augustine as quoted by Thomas, "I perceive that not only can suffering for the name of Christ supply for what is lacking in baptism, but even faith and conversion of heart, if perchance on account of the stress of the times the celebration of the mystery of baptism is not practicable" (*ST* III, q. 66, a. 11;II-II, q. 2, a. 5, ad 1; III, q. 61, a. 1). In its own context Augustine's remark relates only to an evangelized but unbaptized person of good faith.

On the necessity of church membership and juridical subjection to the pope, there is some ambivalence in the writings of St. Thomas. He clearly allows for situations in which salutary faith is available in some implicit manner without actual membership in the church and subjection to the pope. In one place he affirms that "there is no entering salvation outside the Church, just as in the time of the deluge there was none outside the ark which denotes the Church according to I Peter 2:20, 21" (*ST* III, q. 73, a. 3). In the case of the child lost in a European forest, however, he says that God would "most certainly reveal to him (or her) the matter that must be believed," if that child, on reaching the age of discretion, "follows the lead of natural reason in the desire to do good and avoid evil" (*De Veritate* q. 14, a. 11, ad 1).

Given the limited world view of his time and place, it is understandable that Thomas would identify faith with the beliefs of Christians, and that his hypothetical case would not envisage all the unbaptized inhabitants of the much larger and more numerous forests outside the walls of ancient Christendom. However, in his discussion of the incarnation of the divine Logos and the significance of Christ as the Savior of every human being (cf. 1 Tm 4:10; 1 Jn 2:2), Thomas recognizes explicitly the universal sufficiency and ubiquity of "Christ's power" through which "the unbaptized, though not actually in the Church, are in the Church potentially" (*ST* III, q. 8, a. 2, ad 1).

In the debates about the possible salvation or damnation of the strange peoples reportedly living in remote regions newly discovered or rediscovered, like Cathay, the Indus Valley or the territories beyond Ethiopia, Dante Alighieri (1265–1321) appears more optimistic and less cautious than the professional theologians of his time, as we see from these lines of his *Paradiso*:

A man is born on the shores of the river Indus, and there is no one to tell him of Christ. . . . All his desires and deeds are good, so far as human reason sees, sinless in life or speech. He dies unbaptized and without faith. Where is that justice that condemns him? (Canto 19, vv 70–78).

Into the faces of those who would restrict saving grace to the church's visible members, Dante flings these challenging words: "Now who are you to sit in judgment from a thousand miles away. . . ? To this kingdom never ascended anyone who did not believe in Christ. . . . But see, many cry 'Christ! Christ!' who at the last judgment shall be further away from him than many who knew him not" (ibid.).[1]

More than poetry was needed to counter the juridical and pessimistic understanding, axiomatic and canonized, of the church's necessity for everyone's salvation. The official teaching was reiterated more vigorously than ever by Dante's contemporary, Pope Boniface VIII, at the beginning of the fourteenth century. While engaged in a power struggle with Philip IV of France, Boniface affirmed and professed without qualification that, as with the ark of Noah, so also "outside the one . . . Catholic Church there is neither salvation nor remission of sins." As though this were not enough, lest he be misunderstood, Boniface went on with pontifical emphasis: "Furthermore, we declare, say, define and proclaim to every creature that they, by necessity for salvation, are entirely subject to the Roman Pontiff" (Denzinger 1957, nos. 468–69).

The Council of Ferrara and Florence in the following century reaffirmed this position in equally strong and clear language announcing to the world (their world of 1438–45) that "those not living within the Catholic Church, not only pagans but also Jews and heretics and schismatics, cannot become participants in eternal life, but will depart into everlasting fire . . . unless before the end of life the same have been added to the flock" (Denzinger 1957, no. 714).[2]

A literalistic and excessively juridicial understanding of such teachings inspired numerous zealots of damnation and perverted the attitudes of countless Christians in relation to the other communities of faith. A rational hermeneutical method would attempt to explain these papal and conciliar statements in terms of the historico-culture situations and ideological fixations from which they emerged.

Boniface, who annulled all the official acts of his immediate predecessor and confined the unfortunate ex-pope for the remainder of his life, was using the spiritual power of the papacy to assert his "divine" authority over kings and princes. He was thinking more of the political than the theological implications of his statement. Likewise, to understand the message of the Council of Ferrara and Florence, the historical context of the conciliar deliberations would have to be consulted, taking account of such factors as the council's specific concern with the schismatic Coptic community of Egypt, perhaps also the long history of Christian conflicts with Islam, as well as the general cultural isolation of the church within the walls of ancient Christendom with its vast and very slowly dissipating geographic and demographic ignorance concerning the rest of the world (cf. Drummond 1985: 45, 51).

Whatever the blinding forces of culture and history may have been, the expressed teaching of Boniface and Ferrara-Florence hardly reflect the same hopeful good news of salvation that such theologians as Nicholas of Cusa (1401–64) and Juan de Lugo (1583–1616) managed to retain from the earlier tradition. These two, among others, had a keen appreciation not only of the theological implications of saving grace for all of humankind, but also an understanding of the historicity and cultural embeddedness of every person, hence also the possible salutary significance of whatever philosophical or religious systems may be available, however imperfectly, as instruments of God's self-revelation.

The reemergence of a hopeful and positive attitude toward people belonging to other faith communities was very slow in coming, although the Council of Trent (1545–63) had accepted the idea of baptism of desire as an efficacious way of grace for those who, through no fault of their own, had no knowledge of Christ and no access to the church's baptism of water. Yet the zeal of missionaries, like St. Francis Xavier, was fired by the vision of masses of people falling into hell because they had not been baptized. Most missionaries tend to modify their views on this, as Xavier did, in the course of their field experience, as they encounter increasing numbers of thoroughly decent and compassionate non-Christians. By the time Matteo Ricci arrived in China (1583) and Roberto de Nobili in India (1606), a more positive orientation was developing among Jesuit missionaries with respect to both the reality of grace outside the church and the respect due to the cultures of non-European peoples. Nevertheless, even their evaluations of indigenous religions in China and in India were not entirely free of Mediterranean ethnocentrism.

The correct understanding of the axiom "no salvation outside the church" was a recurring topic of ecclesiastical debate, as each generation had its share of theologians, missionaries and pastors who felt "that grace would no longer be grace, if God became too free with it" (Rahner *NG*:31). In an effort to settle the matter once and for all, Pius IX (pope from 1846 to 1878) said:

It must . . . be held as certain that those who are affected by ignorance of the true religion, if it is invincible ignorance, are not subject to any guilt in this matter before the eyes of the Lord. Now, then, who could presume in himself an ability to set the boundaries of such ignorance, taking into consideration the natural differences of peoples, lands, native talents, and so many other factors? . . . The gifts of heavenly grace will surely not be denied to those who sincerely want and pray for refreshment by the divine light.

The pope was mistaken only in his expectation that this clarification would be the final word on the subject. He concluded by saying that "to proceed with further investigation is wrong" (Denzinger 1957, nos. 1647–48).

By the first quarter of the twentieth century it was widely recognized that, nineteen-hundred years after the founding of the church at Pentecost, an ever-increasing percentage of the world's population still lived *extra ecclesiam*, with the church's visible membership progressively diminishing in relation to all the non-members. Even then a famous French Jesuit theologian teaching in Rome, Cardinal Louis Billot, was still using the limbo theory to explain the eternal destiny of all who died in good faith but juridically outside the church. By the middle of this century the American Jesuit Leonard Feeney still persisted in proclaiming the earlier narrow teaching that all are lost who do not belong explicitly to the Roman Catholic Church.

Most theologians, by this time, had moved well beyond the earlier juridicism, as they spoke of the reality of grace outside the church relating non-Christians somehow to the "soul of the church" by means of an "implicit desire" to do all that God would have them do, even though they may not know just what he wants of them. Pope Pius XII, with some cautious hedging in his encyclical letter *Mystici Corporis* had already addressed the question of membership, and how non-Christians might be united to the church "by some unconscious yearning and desire." But the declaration of the Holy Office, which ironically put Leonard Feeney juridically outside the church for insisting that salvation was possible only inside, was about the clearest statement made up to that time by ecclesiastical officialdom:

> To gain eternal salvation it is not always required that a person be incorporated in fact as a member of the Church, but it is required that he belong to it at least in desire and longing. . . . When a man is invincibly ignorant, God accepts an implicit desire, so called because it is contained in the good intentions of soul by which a man wants his will to be conformed to God's will (*The Church Teaches*, 1955, nos. 274–75).

After centuries of ecclesiastical double-talk—"Yes, there is salvation outside the church; but no, there is not"—the leading theologians of Vatican II finally gave up on the ancient axiom that had occasioned so much misunderstanding. "That old formula," says Yves Congar, "should frankly be abandoned, since it cannot be properly understood, except by glossing it in such a way that we make it express something different from what it obviously expresses." All who had interpreted the formula in the rigid manner of St. Cyprian were wrong. In Congar's words, "It is forbidden now to interpret it in the sense given to it by its author" (Congar 1965:59).

RETRIEVING THE AUTHENTIC TRADITION

The retrieval of hopeful insights from the earliest days of Christian theologizing was, as we have noted, tedious and grudging. But the way was prepared for the Second Vatican Council's positive, hence unprecedented, approach to all the faith communities usually designated negatively as non-Christian religions. What at first seemed like speculative novelties created by progressive theologians were really restatements in contemporary terms of an original tradition that had been arrested and marginalized for reasons best described as historico-cultural conditioning.

The creative theologians who, in the decades prior to Vatican II, contributed significantly to this new flowering of an authentically Christian understanding of the graced condition of humanity were themselves sometimes marginalized by the very functionaries responsible for maintaining the orthodoxy of Christian belief. The works of some of this century's greatest theologians (for example, Henri de Lubac, Yves Congar, Karl Rahner, Edward Schillebeeckx) were, as the saying went in those days, "frowned upon by Rome." Since thumbscrews and the rack had been outlawed by secular authorities, this usually meant that such theologians were silenced: not allowed to publish, teach or lecture. Another technique sometimes used against them was the general smear compaign which, without actually naming individual theologians, much less citing the chapters and verses of their alleged deviations from "sound doctrine," cast doubt upon the competence of their scholarship and the integrity of their faith.

Karl Rahner, for example, was harassed for more than a decade before Vatican II. Strenuous efforts made in high places would have prevented his appointment as a Council theologian (*peritus*) had not Cardinals Frings, König and Döpfner brought the matter to the attention of Pope John XXIII, who then made the appointment himself (Vorgrimler 1986:87–94, 148–53).

The newly recovered optimism concerning the universality and superabounding nature of God's self-communication owes much to the creative scholarship of Henri de Lubac and Yves Congar in the pre-conciliar period when both of them were silenced. Also before the Council, but under the protection of Holland's theologically literate Cardinal Alfrink, Edward Schillebeeckx was wrestling with the meaning of God's saving grace in relation to the whole of humankind. All are "already essentially redeemed in principle," he said then in a book on the mother of Jesus (Schillebeeckx 1964:61–62). In his work on sacramentality he put it this way: "The present universal order of human existence is a supernatural order: man is created for Christ (Col 1:16); no fully human personal moral orientation is possible without immediately being implicitly an orientation for or against the *Deus Salutaris*" (Schillebeeckx 1953:7).

This is also a fundamental and recurring theme in the theology of Karl

Rahner who, also on the eve of Vatican II, expressed it precisely and succinctly in these terms:

> Actual human nature is never "pure" nature, but nature in a super-natural order, which man (even the unbeliever and the sinner) can never escape from; nature superformed (which does not mean justi-fied) by the supernatural saving grace offered to it. And these "existential facts" of his concrete (his "historical") nature are not just accidents of his being beyond his consciousness but make themselves apparent in his experience of himself (*NG*:35).[3]

In his or her existential situation within a particular historico-cultural matrix each person is constituted, and transcendentally differentiated from the rest of mundane creation, precisely in his or her freely given capacity for grace as God's loving self-communication. Human beings are what they are because of this capacity to hear and respond to a word from the dimensions of the eternal (Tillich). However ambiguous the realm of human freedom may be in this economy, and in spite of each person's consistently ambivalent exercise of freedom, God's gift of grace is much more effective unto life than are all of humankind's sins and stupidities unto death. "The free gift following many offenses brings jus-tification," as St. Paul said in his letter to the Romans: "So from the justice of one the result is unto justification of life for all per-sons. . . . Where sin increased, grace abounded all the more" (Rom 5:12–21; 11:32). "Once and for all" Christ appeared for the destruction of the sins of all (Heb 9:26–28): one man standing adequately "for all" (2 Cor 5:15), "the just one for the unjust" (1 Pt 3:18).

In the light of this scriptural witness and the numerous other texts sup-porting the optimism of the earliest theologians cited in this chapter, and considering how relatively few human beings have been or will ever be confronted with the gospel message, and mindful of the truth that the magnanimous ways of God, far from the ways of humans, are largely hidden in the depths of divine wisdom (cf. Rom 11:33; 1 Cor 2:7, 12), it follows that "grace works for the most part anonymously" (Rahner *MG* 1:91; cf. *TI* 14:178; cf. *GS* 22).

God's unceasing concern for his creation, which he makes and recreates with equal ease, as also his ever-active interventions in history, are con-cealed in the darkness of faith; they are always subject to misinterpretation by those who would try to measure and to place logical limits upon the magnanimity of God. But his greatness is not less beyond the borders of Israel (Mal 1:5), whether the new Israel or the old: " 'Are not you like the Ethiopians to me, O people of Israel?' says the Lord. 'Did I not bring up Israel from the land of Egypt, and the Philistines from Caphtor and the Syrians from Kir?' " (Am 9:7). Indeed, as St. Paul said to the Athenians at the Areopogus, God made all the peoples on the face of the earth, allotting their respective boundaries of time and place, "that they should seek God in the hope that they might feel after him and find him," although he is not far from anyone (cf. Acts 17:24–28).

THE ANONYMOUS CHRISTIAN

If grace works for the most part anonymously always and everywhere, and if all grace is given on account of Christ (cf. Acts 4:12; Rom 5:15–18; 8:32; 2 Cor 5:15; 1 Tm 2:5), then Rahner's theory of the "anonymous Christian" is well-founded on the most traditional Christian belief in the eternal Logos who enlightens everyone who comes into the world (Jn 1: 9), who finally emerged from creation itself (cf. Is 45: 8) and became historically present, as all real human beings do, in the physical flesh of a definite ethnic group and within the context of a particular culture during a brief time span.

Whether one approaches Christology "from above" or "from below,"[4] the unique relationship between God and Jesus of Nazareth is central to the whole belief system of Christians. The relationship is traditionally understood in terms of the incarnation. Theologians in every age have tried to explicate this belief in ways that are plausible, if not fully intelligible, to the Christians of their respective times and cultural matrices. As with all objective religious beliefs, however rigorously defined in abstract philosophical propositions, the concrete understanding and application must always be subjective, because the understanding and application is always and only done by a particular, contingent and historically conditioned subject who is confined to this or that time, place and cultural frame of reference with its peculiar assumptions, ideologies and biases. No mortals achieve the objectivity of a divine vantage point. Even Jesus was as circumscribed as the rest of us by his human situation, conditioned by the particularity of time, place and culture. We may assume, for example, that he shared the erroneous geographical and cosmological views of his contemporaries. Otherwise, if he had been secretly relying on divinely supplied information, he would not have been truly human, a Jew of his own time in everything except sin; nor would he be an honest model for humankind. Invincible ignorance, hence inculpable errors, belong universally to the human condition. Even scripture is a witness to the ignorance of Jesus (cf. Rahner *TI* 16:188–89, 241).

From a specifically Western Christian viewpoint in the second half of the twentieth century, and in terms of the traditional Christian belief system—but not from the particular vantage point of a Hindu, Buddhist, Jew or Muslim—it is appropriate to think of non-Christians who respond to God's grace as "anonymous Christians." It is hard not to regard them thus, although this is another less-than perfect way of expressing the traditional belief in the universal reality of saving grace. This grace, Christians generally believe with St. Paul, is given on account of Christ who is the divine Word-made-flesh and the only mediator between God and humankind.

They also believe that they themselves have been called by God and gathered into the church precisely in order to be sent out in the name of Christ for the continuation of his mission to all of humankind in its historical extension, ethnic diversity and cultural plurality.

So it is also appropriate to think of all who respond to grace as belonging implicitly to the church by "some unconscious yearning and desire," as Pope Pius XII said, thereby moving the discussion forward in his time. All such expressions refer to the same belief that ancient theologians explained in terms of the church existing "from the time of Abel." Tertullian of Carthage in the third century was articulating this same belief when he spoke of morally upright unbelievers whose souls were "naturally Christian" (quoted in de Lubac 1967:71).

Karl Barth explicates this belief in terms of the "concealed and dormant people of God in the world" (Barth 1956:418). Paul Tillich, in turn, describes Christian missionary activity as the means by which the church works "for the transformation of its own latency into its own manifestation all over the world. . . .This transformation is one from the Church in its latency, in its hiddenness under the forms of paganism, Judaism, and humanism, into its manifestation" (Tillich 1961:183, 285).

None of these theologians claims that the "naturally Christian soul," or the "anonymous Christian," or the "latent church," embraces every single person who lives visibly outside the community of Christian belief. Still it could be argued, with appropriate explanations, that every human being may be regarded as a Christian insofar as the church stands in sacramental symbolism for the whole of humankind who are, whether they all know it or not, God's own people, created in his image and redeemed by the grace of Christ.

While we may have a firm hope in the salvation of everyone, God alone knows who actually responds to his gift of friendship, which is adequately available to persons outside as well as inside the visible structures of the church. According to a well-known saying of St. Augustine, many who appear to be outside the church are truly inside, and many who seem to be inside are really outside. Those on the outside who respond to the grace that is offered on account of Christ may be called "anonymous Christians."[5] We cannot know how numerous such "Christians" may be, any more than we can know how many of the church's juridical members are authentic Christians. But, as Christians, we do believe that, in spite of the ambiguity of human freedom and a great capacity for choosing wrongly and acting stupidly, "the redemptive grace of 'Christus Victor,' " as Edward Schillebeeckx reminds us, "is more powerful than the fragility of human freedom" (Schillebeeckx 1965:49–50).

Karl Rahner's exposition of the workings of grace has found wide acceptance among theologians, especially in the Catholic tradition, although some have reservations about some of his emphases and also about the expression "anonymous Christian." Without using these terms, Pope John

Paul II certainly reflects Rahner's theology of grace in these lines of his encyclical letter, *Redemptor Hominis*: "The human person—every person without any exception whatever—has been redeemed by Christ; and Christ is in a way united with each person, without any exception whatever, even when they are not aware of this" (no. 14; cf. no. 13). Again, St. Paul's address to the Athenians comes to mind. What they worshiped as unknown (implicit/anonymous), Paul proclaimed (made explicit/named) in their hearing (cf. Acts 17:23).

QUESTIONS OF TERMINOLOGY

In response to the critics of his terminology (notable theologians like Hans Küng and John Macquarrie, for example), who feel that "anonymous Christian" smacks of the same old Christian imperialism that has long been a barrier to authentic dialogue with the followers of other religions, Rahner has persistently defended his use of the expression: "Whoever thinks that the term 'implicit Christianity' should be avoided is free to do so. He must just offer another term which describes the situation as clearly and briefly. The same must be said for the cognate term 'anonymous Christianity'" (*AC*:43).[6]

One might add that an insistence upon universally acceptable religious terminology, lest anyone be disturbed or offended, should also preclude the word *God* in theological discussions that might be overheard by atheists, or by the non-theists in certain types of Hinduism and Buddhism. Nor would it be appropriate, in the hearing of Muslims, to speak of three divine persons. Such restrictions would render honest dialogue, which can be disturbing to Christians as well as to the others, impossible.

Frederick E. Crowe and Wilfred Cantwell Smith, while accepting Rahner's meaning, have suggested ways of avoiding the objectionable connotations of his historically and culturally specific, hence exclusivistic, terminology. Instead of "anonymous Christian," Smith finds "anonymous Christianity" less objectionable. Since the term *Christian* was coined in Antioch to describe the people of the new religious "way" (Acts 9:2; 11:26), Crowe proposes coining another descriptive word for all who, in responding to grace, receive the Holy Spirit as the first, basic and universal consequence of God's will that every one should be saved. "Until we can find a better term," he suggests "anonymous Spiritains," although this also belongs to one historically specific religious tradition (Crowe 1984:18–19).

Smith proposes the elimination altogether of the word *Christian*, as it is not a theological term but a historically descriptive one. God's universal offer of grace, when accepted existentially (or when not rejected) results in faith. It is faith, not anonymous Christianity, that is shared by all who, whatever the historico-cultural religion available to them, respond to (or do not reject) the grace offered to all. Moving beyond St. Paul's vision of Christian unity in which there is "neither Jew nor Greek . . . neither male nor female," (Gal 3:28), Smith says that among persons united to God by faith "there are neither Christians nor Muslims nor others; for we are all one in being offered grace, and potentially one in accepting it" (Smith 1984:68).

Rahner himself was speaking in these very terms in 1974, as he argued that even atheists can make a genuine act of faith (without which no one is saved). This happens when persons freely and unconditionally accept themselves for what they really are in their radical, even if unthematized, reference to God who is always present to all. The person's free acceptance of this supernatural finality, even without conscious reflection upon it, is an act of faith in response to grace, which works for the most part anonymously. So "there exists what we term 'anonymous faith.' " How this relates to explicit Christianity is explained by Rahner:

If during his life a person is offered, in a manner which is credible to him, the chance to give objective structure and shape to his being (and therefore an opportunity of supernatural elevation), and if he rejects this possibility, then he is deliberately denying his grace-filled transcendence as well. It is not possible to have "anonymous faith" when its thematic expression in the Christian belief in revelation is culpably rejected. But as long as a person is not guilty of this and at the same time accepts himself in a moral decision, he assumes at the same time his own radical transcendence, which is ordered to the direct presence of God, and so possesses anonymous faith (*TI* 16:58–59).

To indicate the same reality frequently called "anonymous Christianity" by Rahner, Bernard Lonergan also favors the use of "faith" as a theologically acceptable way of facilitating ecumenical discourse (Lonergan 1972:123). Lonergan prefers the religious neutrality of abstract philosophical terms such as "differentiation and transformation of consciousness" and "self-transcendence." Such terms provide a religiously neutral way of speaking about the common human phenomenon of unthematized religious conversion experienced, but not culturally objectified in a particular belief system, in consequence of God's love proffered to every person.

The common language needed for adequate interreligious dialogue among persons currently separated by their respective historico-cultural experiences will be found only progressively as a global consciousness of religious community emerges from the wider ecumenism. So we must move forward, however haltingly, with mutual respect and earnest efforts to grasp the inner meanings of the particular terms of humankind's multiple religious ways of expressing a common faith.

THE COMMON WAY

More important than any formula or label used for a contemporary understanding of the ubiquity of saving grace is the manner in which this grace is proffered to every human being and the ways through which it may be freely accepted or rejected. How, then, are we to picture the relationship between the daily activities of people and the action of grace? The domains of nature and grace are not separated in the way that the first and second storeys of a house are separated and capable of being used as two distinctly different apartments with some people living above in a supernatural state and others remaining below on a merely natural level, or the same people sometimes living upstairs and sometimes down, in one state or the other. Nor is the first storey to be seen as a base for the second. Grace presupposes nature and operates only through the terms of nature. Nature itself exists for the sake of, or because of, God's self-communication which is called grace. Although they are distinguishable, nature and grace exist for each other. "There cannot be any grace," says Rahner, "which does not imply a quite definite putting into action of nature; nor can there be any human, responsible putting of nature into action which is not subject to the demands of grace, amounting *in concreto*, with no avoidance of it while life lasts, to a Yes or No to grace." So, when all is said and done, real grace exists only in *persons graced*, or nature graced as a divinization of precisely *that* "nature" (*MG* 1:63).

The moments of grace, above all and more frequently than we like to think, occur in ordinary situations involving the needs of others. God offers himself/herself to everyone in those unplanned events that break in upon us, interrupt us, disturb us, challenge us, and demand from us a decisive answer. Human destiny in relation to God and the ultimate meaning of our lives is brought to fulfillment in these salutary historical events impinging upon us directly and relentlessly. Dietrich Bonhoeffer perceived these events as "interruptions by God constantly crossing our paths and cancelling our plans, by sending us people with claims and petitions" (Bonhoeffer 1954:89). Good intentions and lofty aspirations may be formed, and the works of grace may be celebrated in churches, temples and groves; but the really decisive encounters with God are commonly made elsewhere – primarily "where good is promoted and evil is fought against for the healing of humanity" (Schillebeeckx 1987:9). Gregory Baum puts it this way:

The divine summons empowering people to enter into holiness does not thereby lift them out of their historical situation and make them ready for an invisible world, but leaves them in their historical place and appoints them to be agents of Christ in their troubled societies (Baum 1979:55).

In the final analysis St. Matthew's account of the last judgment to be faced by every human being may be taken as normative for all Christian theologizing about salvation anywhere and at any time, inside or outside the convenants of biblical revelation, with or without the help of traditional belief systems and ecclesiastical doctrines (cf. Mt 25: 31–46). It is noteworthy in this story that those who responded positively to saving grace, which was offered only in reference to the real needs of others, did not explicitly recognize Christ. He was efficaciously present to them, but only anonymously in "ten thousand faces not his own," as Gerard Manley Hopkins reminds us in a famous poem.

On the basis of this judgment story it may be seen that grace is not made available primarily in rituals, readings, homilies, retreats, laws, prayers, hymns, processions, and so forth. However important such actions may be for personal reflection, the celebration of faith, the expression of belief, and thus for focusing ourselves symbolically upon the real order of Christian priorities, they remain secondary occasions of grace. It is in the common and ordinary events of daily life that the drama of salvation and damnation takes place. At the most elementary level this happens when persons obey or disobey the dictates of conscience, which usually coincide with the dictates of reason enlightened by faith and aided by any other guidance available in the present order of human existence, which is itself superformed, or continuously re-created by God's loving presence and superabounding self-communication.

The action of grace occurs unthematically when, for example, a human being accepts the inevitable fact of death as appropriate, as normal destiny, for one who exists only contingently, from beginning to end, in any plausible order of existence. As a final occasion of grace, it is the destiny of everyone to experience death, and the vast majority who suffer this experience have never heard the name of Jesus. Another common encounter with grace, as illustrated by Karl Rahner, is in the natural act of loving another person:

> When, for example, a concrete human being (and whether he is aware of it or not is, in the first instance, immaterial) experiences genuine, personal love for another human being, it always has a validity, an eternal significance and an inexpressible depth which it would not have but that such a love is so constituted as to be a way of actualizing the love of God as a human activity springing from God's own act (*MG* 1:79).

Why so much? Why take so seriously and see so much of ultimate significance in such commonplace events as the mundane experiences of death and love? The Christian answer: because humankind is made in the image and likeness of God who so loves us that, in the Incarnation of the divine Word, he (or she or it) deigns to experience fully this human mode of existence outside the Godhead. God thus communicates in an earthly manner, by means of culturally fashioned symbols and contingent events, with all of humankind, becoming "in every way" one of us in the tangible terms of human history, flesh, finitude, "even tasting death for every one," so that all might be recognized as members of one family reconciled, restored, reunited (cf. Heb 2: 2–18).

Real saints are not distinguishable from the rest of us by the intensity, frequency or multiplicity of their religious practices but by the extent of their unfeigned human decency, normally expressed and commonly recognized by such acts as compassion, generosity, fairness, forgiveness and forbearance.

Sanctity for humans is a matter of becoming like God, having been constituted in the divine image. But this process of divinization through grace is the work of a lifetime. It is a comfort to know, anyway, that when we do not knowingly reject grace, we accept it. This is true not only of believing Christians but of every human being (cf. Rahner *FC*:1343, 429–30; Fuchs 1970:69; *GS* 2, 10, 22). This is obviously a matter of fundamental importance for the church's new relationship to non-Christian religions; it is also a basic assumption for the world-mission of a church that aspires to become authentically catholic (cf. Rahner *TI* 20:82).

VATICAN COUNCIL II

The theology of grace, as expounded particularly by Rahner, Congar, de Lubac and Schillebeeckx, is reflected throughout the documents of the Second Vatican Council. By returning to a broader understanding of the church's sacramentality, the Council's soteriology became significantly more Christocentric, or less ecclesiocentric, than that of theologians enjoying the official approval of the Council's preparatory commission under the firm guidance of Cardinal Ottaviani's Holy Office. By rejecting the older metaphor of the church as a plank of salvation for a shipwrecked humanity, and by retrieving the theology of the church as the sacrament (symbol, sign, witness, token, pledge) of the salvation of the whole world, the perennial confusion concerning the meaning and necessity of the church was finally removed. In the teaching of Vatican II, says Karl Rahner, "the salvific will of God . . . is proclaimed as so universal and effective that it can be restricted only by a person's decision made with a bad conscience and at no other point" (*TI* 20:82, 100).

This illuminating breakthrough occurred early in the conciliar deliberations on the nature of the church; it occurred, according to Karl Rahner, "quietly and spontaneously, without opposition, without surprise" (*CF*:82). Through a long and wearisome process the pessimism of St. Augustine regarding salvation was gradually dismantled in the course of centuries and finally superseded by the more hopeful soteriology of Vatican II. Not only did the Council quietly inter the old "limbo" doctrine; it "boldly postulated a revelation properly so called, and consequently a real opportunity of faith even where the Christian message had not been proclaimed; it did not regard even the profession of atheism as unambiguous proof that a person could not be saved—which certainly is not in agreement with the traditional teaching before the Council" (Rahner *TI* 20:100–1).

In the documents of Vatican II, moreover, the church is not presented as the society of those who are more favored or given a better chance of salvation; much less is it the gathering of those who alone are saved. It is a community of witnesses chosen not for themselves, but for others, for the non-church. In Rahner's words, "the Church is . . . the sign of the salvation of those who, as far as its historical and social structure are concerned, do not belong to it." The broad theological significance of the church's self-understanding, as articulated by Vatican II, is further elaborated by Rahner:

The Church is the tangible, historical manifestation of the grace in which God communicates himself as absolutely present, close and forgiving, of the grace which is at work everywhere, omits no one, offers God to each and gives to every reality in the world a secret purposeful orientation towards the intrinsic glory of God (*CF*:83).

The significance of the church for humankind's salvation was thus clarified by a fresh emphasis upon the universality and efficacy of the grace of Christ outside the structures of the church. While insisting upon the necessity of visible church membership for persons who were adequately confronted with the gospel message, and thus called to become Christ's witnesses among the nations, the same possibility of sanctification and salvation for everyone else, in virtue of the same grace of Christ, was given due emphasis. God, who is not far from anyone, in his own ways leads to himself those who are inculpably ignorant of the gospel. He leads them to that faith without which it is impossible to please him (Cf. Heb 11:6; *AG* 3, 7; *LG* 14–16; *GS* 2, 10, 22; *NA* 1).

The final word in a chapter on the universality of grace, as a prelude to considering the possibilities of a much wider ecumenism than previously contemplated by Christians, must be left to Karl Rahner:

In more than a millennium of struggle, theology has overcome Augustinian pessimism in regard to the salvation of the individual and reached the optimism of the Second Vatican Council, assuring supernatural salvation in the immediate possession of God to all those who do not freely reject it through their own personal fault; our question now must be whether theology can regard the non-Christian religions with the same optimism (*TI* 18:291).

3

Toward A Wider Ecumenism

To prepare the way for a wider ecumenism than what we have been experiencing in recent years as an ecumenical dialogue among separated Christians, the various elements for a contemporary Christian theology of religion may be brought together on the common ground of faith. The gift of faith, as understood in the two preceding chapters (where faith is not simply identified with the beliefs of Christians), initiates humankind's union with the ineffable ground of all reality, or the ultimate meaning of reality, designated in many religious traditions by the theological shorthand term *God*. This union (healing, integration, liberation, *nirvana*, salvation, *mukti*), or an unreflexive (not yet objectified in the symbols of a particular culture) longing for it, is experienced in faith only vaguely and preconceptually, in a dark manner or unthematically, as appropriate human destiny, or as the final meaning of mundane existence within a universe that is culturally ordered, hence rationally plausible.

Faith, seeking expression in the cultural worlds of real people, gives rise to foundational religious beliefs and practices consciously and thematically articulated through culturally devised symbols and categories dealing explicitly with the meaning of human experiences, observations, longings and anxieties. Beliefs and practices are thus developed regarding, for example, the ways of achieving destiny, seeking the meaning of human existence, avoiding the pitfalls labelled sin or evil, and tempering the sting of death. While all such beliefs and practices are rooted in a common faith available to every human person, they are culturally fashioned and historically circumscribed, and thus particularized, because humankind exists only within countless communities differentiated profoundly by the particularities of culture and of ethnicity, and because humankind exists only in the consecutive terms of a gradually unfolding and ever-changing human history.

So it is that the world is replete with myriad faith communities or religions "found everywhere, striving variously to answer the restless searchings of the human heart, by proposing 'ways' which consist of teachings, rules of life, and sacred ceremonies" (*NA* 2). A person's socially constructed,

45

culturally colored, historically conditioned and faith-illumined religious experience—not excluding, of course, other realms of experience in the present supernatural order of human existence—mediates his or her transcendental nature and self-understanding both individually as one who freely disposes of one's self, and socially as one relates inescapably and variously to his or her particular community of destiny with its inevitably limited horizons.

INSTRUMENTS OF GRACE AND EXPRESSIONS OF FAITH

Before the Second Vatican Council (1962–65) most of the Christian theologizing about the availability of saving grace outside the visible structures of the church took relatively little positive account of non-Christian faith communities. Instead, the concern was mainly with human beings considered individually. Inadequate attention was given to the historical, social and cultural conditioning of human existence in the real world. Human nature was understood too abstractly. So there was a disincarnate and ahistorical quality to the discussions about individual cases.[1] There was, moreover, an apologetical anxiety about the necessity of church membership and belief correctly formulated. These were deemed the "ordinary" means of salvation for everyone. Being outside was assumed to be the exception rather than the rule. Most of the world's population was conceptually consigned to an "extraordinary" situation *vis-a-vis* God's saving will. Extra-biblical religions were generally dismissed as merely natural at best, satanic at worst.

There were, however, always some theologians with a historical consciousness and cultural sensitivity enabling them to appreciate the full significance of the pluriform and ever-changing sociocultural matrices and historical time frames within which human lives are lived inescapably. Karl Rahner and Edward Schillebeeckx were among those trying to take full account of the meaning and implications of the incarnation of the divine Logos, as God's way of communicating with humankind through a historical event realized in the physical and cultural flesh of a particular ethnic group, and expressed in the religious terms of their concrete faith community during a moment of their history.

The whole biblical story of God's approaches to humankind is clearly incarnational and dialogical and historically conditioned. The "good news" entrusted to the Lord's followers must be communicated through the particular linguistic and religious symbol systems historically available to the peoples for whom the gospel is intended. Considering what it is to be human in the dimensions of time and place, there seems no other way of effectively communicating, representing and celebrating the meaning of Christianity. The incarnation of the divine Word is not just a hopeful belief for the edification of Christians; it is also an action model for the mission entrusted to them.

In Jesus of Nazareth God's "good news" was not presented through alien linguistic and religious systems brought down from heaven. The message came through the flesh of a particular ethnic group; it was verbalized in a provincial dialect intelligible to the people on the spot; it was expounded in metaphors fashioned from the experiences of shepherds and fishermen against a background of preconceptions and assumptions that were hardly universal. The new faith community that emerged was seen, expressed and celebrated in full continuity with the pre-Christian history, language and religion of those who were called in order to be sent to others in the lands beyond. If God communicates with his creatures in the less-than-perfect terms of this one particular faith community of Israel, why not also through all the other religions that have always served and continue to serve an ever-increasing majority of the world's population? If the religion of Israel could be an authentic instrument of God's saving grace, why not all the others?

The answer given before Vatican II by Edward Schillebeeckx, on the basis of insights attributed to Thomas Aquinas, is this:

A religion founded purely on philosophical insight, "natural religion" based on that which the unaided human spirit can achieve of itself, is a fiction, metaphysically impossible in fact, because the *eidos* of religion, as phenomenologically established in the analysis of the universally human fact of religion, necessarily implies personal relations between God and humans, and these clearly cannot be achieved by the created powers of humans alone.

In the concrete all religion presupposes an at least anonymous supernatural revelation and faith. There is thus, anterior to any Judeo-Christian religion, an *instinctus divinus* arising from the deepest foundations of human religious psychology as influenced by the attraction of divine grace (Schillebeeckx 1963:8 n. 2).

It follows that the historical development of religious systems, variously articulating a living faith among diverse peoples, and expressing in beliefs, rites and practices their hardly avoidable experience of the ineffable ground of all reality, signifies "an anonymous but nonetheless effective operation of grace" (ibid.). This also explains the appropriateness of early Christianity's original Jewishness and its later assimilation, thanks to St. Paul, of various other Mediterranean religious symbols, concepts, forms, rites and practices into the life of the church. It is the way of incarnation, the only way that God communicates with his creatures of flesh, history and culture.

Just how seriously must these varied historico-cultural religions be taken? Given Christianity's long and wide absence to most of humanity in the course of history, after as well as before Christ's visible advent in the flesh and in the sacramentality of the church, it is not surprising that the inner workings of grace among peoples always and everywhere should have become manifest in a multitude of religions. To deny any salutary signifi-cance to all these forms and structures would be analogous to denying any intelligibility to the proliferating languages of humankind. It would also amount to a denial of the essentially social nature of human existence. Can we Christians, who insist upon the historical nature and social structure of our own faith community, assert that God offers salvation to all non-Chris-tians only as aggregates of individuals separated from, or even in spite of, their collective faith experiences within their respective communities of human destiny?

Just as we are unable, as private linguists, to create a perfect language, but must instead use one that was constructed in the course of generations and is most readily available to us in our particular temporal and social situation, so also, as private metaphysicians, we cannot invent a perfect religion but must normally use the one at hand in our own limited time and place. If one can inwardly experience and outwardly express one's divinely given faith only through the historico-cultural terms of a concrete society, then one has a right and indeed a duty to correspond positively with this gift within the particular context of the religious and social pos-sibilities that are historically and culturally available (cf. Rahner *TI* 5:131). God, in other words, finds people where they are, not where they are not. He speaks to them through their own cultural symbol systems, not through a foreign system that is hardly available or completely unknown.

If the whole of humankind is made in God's image and included in his universally efficacious will that all should be saved (excepting only those who freely reject God's offer), then we may ask whether or to what extent the religions of the world are a part of the historical processes through which the Creator's ecumenical purpose is being accomplished. Are these religions valid instruments of grace and authentic expressions of faith? Are they in general to be regarded as positive media for orienting people toward a proper relation to God? Are they, in other words, divinely intended means of grace? Can we assume that these religions are, in a manner parallel to the Israelite religion, "positively included in God's plan of salvation," in spite of the inevitable distortions, deviations and corruptions found in them? (Cf. Rahner *TI* 5:125:27).

If persons can always have a saving positive relationship with God, and always had to have this as something that could be frustrated only by their own deliberate and malicious rejection of it, then they had it precisely within the available religion actually at their disposal in their respective existential milieux. It is "within the *concrete* religion" of a person's historico-cultural situation that, "in accordance with God's will and by his permission (no longer adequately separable in practice)," the divinely intended means of salvation for the individual reaches him or her (ibid., 128–29; cf. also *TI* 17, chap. 7; 18 chap. 17).

If this line of thought is credible, and we take account of church mem-bership statistics through the ages, we must assume that most of humankind's saved members, hence also the majority of heaven's population, found salvation outside the visible structures of the church and without having ever heard the name of Jesus. Did the religions historically and culturally available to these people, within the spacio-temporal boundaries allotted to them by God who is not far from anyone (cf. Acts 17:26–28), have nothing at all to do with this? Pietro Rossano of the Vatican Secretariat for Non-Christian Religions is among the theologians who find the teaching of Vatican II "explicit on this point. . . . that the gift of 'grace and truth' do reach or may reach the hearts of men and women through the visible, experiential signs of the various religions" (1983:103).

VATICAN COUNCIL II

The Council's Declaration on Non-Christian Religions (*Nostra Aetate*), while signaling a radical reversal of previous attitudes and a new departure from earlier theological positions, is neither as ample nor as explicit in its exposition of the subject as the theologians cited in this chapter. It should therefore be read against the background of the soteriology of the other conciliar documents, especially *Lumen Gentium*, *Gaudium et Spes*, and *Ad Gentes*. Nevertheless, this document might well be regarded by later historians as the symbol of the Council's single most revolutionary accomplishment. Its implications, if taken seriously, are certainly very far-reaching, raising profound questions not previously examined nor fully debated by theologians about the meaning of the mission of Jesus Christ and concerning the future shape of the church and its ministry among the nations.

The brevity and reticence of *Nostra Aetate* is understandable in the light of its genesis. The initial plan was for a modest conciliar statement aimed at improving Christian attitudes toward the Jewish people. Christianity is, of course, uniquely and indispensably related to Judaism. But Western Christians had also to deal with a long history of anti-Semitism plus some acutely haunting memories and guilt feeling from recent European history. The first effort to produce a statement, politely recognizing the respect due not only to the Jewish faith community but also to all other religions, contained only two lines on the other religions serving two-thirds of the world's population.

This display of Western myopia aroused the attention of the non-Western bishops who were one-third of the Council's members. Their comments on the global significance of the other non-Christian religions, serving vastly greater segments of humanity than Judaism, were a lively reminder of the church's call to be catholic in fact as well as in name. The debate on this topic was an exercise in conciliar consciousness-raising. It was a much-needed affirmation of the church's catholicity against the chronic European ethnocentrism of ecclesiastical officialdom. From then on the Council fathers started to look less like the keepers of a European folk religion and more like the representatives of a world church, if not yet like the promoters of an ecumenical faith community (cf. Stransky 1966:335–48). Without searching out, much less trying to develop, all the implications of their fresh approach to the Christian significance of humankind's religious pluralism, the documents of Vatican II opened the way for further theological exploration along the lines first indicated by some of the earliest fathers of the church, notably Justin Martyr and Clement of Alexandria. In this tradition the various religions may be seen as pluriform reflections of the divine Word's perennial activity in human history; they are understood as "seeds of the Word" — a patristic expression given new prominence by the Council (cf. John Paul II, *RH* no. 11, n. 67).

John Paul II, commenting on "the various non-Christian religions," sees religion as "a universal phenomenon linked with humankind's history." The multiplicity of different faith communities witnesses to "the primacy of the spiritual . . . with direct effects on the whole of culture." Moreover, these flowerings from the "seeds of the Word" attest "that, though the routes taken may be different, there is but a single goal . . . a quest for God . . . and also for the full meaning of human life" (ibid.). Following the lead of the Council, John Paul II also speaks glowingly of "the magnificent heritage of the human spirit that has been manifested in all religions" (ibid., no. 12).

The force of *Nostra Aetate* is in its very positive attitude toward all religions, officially proclaiming a radically changed outlook and repudiating the negative approaches of former times. Going beyond mere rhetoric, the document calls the church to a new venture of "dialogue and collaboration with the followers of the other religions," urging Christians to "acknowledge, preserve and promote the spiritual and moral goods found among these human beings, as well as the values in their society and culture" (*NA* 2). Addressing the missionary implications of this conciliar declaration, John Paul II elaborates upon its meaning, recalling the "missionary attitude" of the apostles and acknowledging the church's past failures in this regard:

> Suffice it to mention St. Paul and, for instance, his address in the Areopagus at Athens. The *missionary* attitude always begins with a deep esteem for "what is in human beings" (Jn 2:25), for what persons have worked out in the depths of the human spirit concerning the most profound and important problems. It is a question of respecting everything that has been brought about in human beings by the Spirit breathing where it wills (Jn 3:8).
>
> The mission is never destruction, but instead is a taking up and fresh building, even if in practice there has not always been full correspondence with this high ideal (*RH* no. 12; cf. also *LG* 17; *AG* 11).

This last line, although obviously an understatement, is a long overdue acknowledgment of the church's faulty approach to non-Western peoples, their cultures and their religions. Unfortunately, "in practice" many missionaries have not yet begun to correspond with the "high ideal" just described. Even many of the local pastoral clergy of the young churches have been slow to accept "in practice" the clear directives of the Council regarding the cultural and religious traditions of their own peoples, opting instead for the continued imitation of a specifically Western experience, expression and celebration of Christianity.

ALL RELIGIONS DEFECTIVE

All religions wear the stains and bear the shame of human inadequacy and sinfulness. As previously noted under the heading "corruptibility" in the first chapter of this book, religious systems, like the cultures in which they subsist, are defective. They may even contain and perpetuate corrupting elements. This must be admitted also of the biblical religions of both the old and the new covenants. We need only recall, for example, the repeated messages of the prophets of Israel, or the perversions known as holy crusades and sacred inquisitions. In our less-than-perfect world even the religious community inspired by belief in the incarnate Word of God and the guidance of the Holy Spirit remains far from a state of eschatological perfection, as we know from modern as well as ancient ecclesiastical history.

With specific reference to this experience of faith in the Roman Catholic community, the septuagenarian biblical scholar John L. McKenzie made this point sharply in a parable about a couple of professional gamblers from a Mississippi River steamboat docked for a few hours in a remote village. On shore they became separated. After some hours one located the other participating in a local card game. After watching for a while, he realized that his companion was engaged in a dishonest game, so he whispered to him "this game is crooked." The companion replied, "I know it's crooked, but it's the only game in town" (McKenzie 1986:17).

The fact that a genuine religion is defective does not generally mean that it is completely depraved, any more than the fact that all human beings are sinners means that human nature is totally vitiated. Nor would the conviction that a religion is a valid instrument of grace imply that its erroneous or malign elements are sanctioned by God, although the weeds and the wheat are usually permitted to grow together until the end. The fallibility and peccability of fallen humankind are reflected in religions no less than in all the other human systems and institutions which can also, in various surprising ways, serve God's purposes. In ancient Egypt, for example, the divine purpose was served by the oppressive Pharaoh's household in which Moses was reared and prepared for the leadership of his people on their long march to freedom (cf. Acts 18:22). But religious structures, more directly than others, are specifically appropriate ways of helping people to go beyond themselves by trying to dispose them for some experiential realization of their transcendent inclinations and aspirations, by proposing answers to questions about the meaning of existence, and by offering ways of coping with the vast unknown.

Religions in themselves, interpreted and administered by sinners, are instruments of grace and manifestations of faith. At the very same time they are dramatic reminders of every person's need for grace. As the fathers of Vatican II remind us—in terms reminiscent of Martin Luther's "saints and sinners at the same time"—the church is "at the same time holy and always in need of being purified" (*LG* 10). Can something like this be said of all religions? Each of them always requires purification of itself through the repentance of its most faithful followers. This implies the humble and honest self-criticism of the faithful believers who must be forever adapting and reforming the human elements of religion in obedience to the inner movements of grace, which is denied to no one.

However inadequate a religion may be, the grace of God remains the same, as does redeemed humankind's capacity for responding to grace in the present supernatural order of existence. God has mercy on whom he will have mercy (cf. Rom 9:14–16). So the possibility remains equally valid for every person to respond, through graced obedience, to the witness of his or her conscience, however conditioned this witness may be by historical circumstances (cf. Rom 2:14–16); for even these circumstances may be determined by God for his own good purposes (cf. Acts 17:26–28; Rom 9:17–18). No religious systems are more important than the persons for whom they exist. Nor are these external means, as culturally created and historically conditioned institutions, more salutary than the inner movements of grace and the longing for God they are supposed to signify, serve and celebrate.

The religions themselves, as instruments, do not actually save people, but they do make people conscious of their need for salvation. Opportunities for accepting God's offer of personal communion, however variously conceptualized or thematized the offer may be, are surely promoted and even provided through the good and positive elements found in all religions: "whatever is true, whatever is honorable, whatever is just, whatever is pure, whatever is lovely, whatever is gracious" (Phil 4:8). Every religion serves God's ecumenical purpose insofar as it offers individuals an awareness of their inadequacies before God, even when the divinity may only be ambiguously sensed as a suspected influence behind the immediate questions of human destiny. Every religious act is a saving act insofar as it disposes persons to a greater love for one another.

COMPARATIVE VALUE OF RELIGIONS

This is not a matter of saying that as a means of helping people along the path that leads to salvation one religion is as good as another, or as bad. There is no objectively reliable evidence for making such comparisons, which are analogous to comparing the value of languages. Sweeping generalizations concerning the comparative humanizing and salutary value of the countless religious systems of humankind, like so much of the grand theorizing in this field (for example, Arnold Toynbee), should be looked upon with considerable reservation, if not downright suspicion. Some of the "precipitate comparisons and indentifications" made by Mircea Eliade, for example, and some of the sources of his data, are questionable (cf. Stransky 1966:53, 87, 138 n. 48). Lacking the divine perspective required for judging comparatively all the values and dis-values, intrinsic and extrinsic, of each religion, we may say simply that each is a different historical means by which, through whatever is good in each, God's saving purpose is served.

Nor is it easily demonstrable that one religion considered either objectively or subjectively is superior to all the others, although Jews, Christians and Muslims tend to regard their respective religions as uniquely superior and pleasing to God. Any religion that is completely foreign to a people's cultural world is like an unknown language to them. For purposes of communication, which is what both religions and languages are essentially about, an unknown symbol system, however sophisticated or even divinely guided, hardly seems as relevant to a people as their own locally integrated system, however haltingly this may express their human experiences and the faith of their particular community.

So both objectively and subjectively the local religion may be seen as more appropriate for a people than an unknown one, although given the constant phenomena of cultural change and interaction with other cultures, foreign beliefs, rites and practices can be harmoniously assimilated and integrated in the course of time through a process of dialogue and incarnation. The communication of the divine Word in the physical flesh and cultural symbol systems of the ancient Jews may be described as incarnational dialogue, "a wonderful exchange," offered in the New Testament as a model process for communication between Christians and the followers of the other religions.

JUDAISM AS PARADIGM

If we are persuaded with St. Paul (cf. Rom 9:4–5; 11:28–29) that the original faith community from which Christianity emerged is more than a mere preparation for Christianity, then the new Israel of the church's self-understanding does not simply supersede and invalidate the old Israel, but must now be understood by Christians more eschatologically in relation to the enduring significance of the Jewish people of God as paradigmatic for the whole human enterprise. "While all the problems have not been solved," says John Pawlikowski in his careful study of this question, "it is necessary to assert that Judaism continues to play a unique and distinctive role in the process of human salvation" (Pawlikowski 1982:121).

If this one faith community is seen as an indispensable precondition for the emergence of the divine Word "once-and-for-all" in the physically and culturally tangible terms of human history, then what about all the other pre-Christian faith communities? Are these also, in ways we have hardly begun to think about, preconditions without which the divine Word (incarnated as the sacrament of God) cannot become present through a community of believers (called to be the sacrament of Christ) in the tangible terms of history and culture among all the other particular peoples who make up and represent symbolically the whole of redeemed humanity? If, moreover, Judaism continues to play a role in the history of salvation after the advent of Jesus Christ, then perhaps the other pre-Christian religions also have a continuing role to play in relation to Christianity.

The history of salvation (grace at work always and everywhere among all peoples) is not outside of human history; it is coextensive with human history. If we believe that God has been lovingly present and active in Israel's history, should we not also believe in the same divine presence among all peoples, the difference being that the recorded religious experiences of the Israelites became part of the Christian heritage, while the records (or non-records) of others did not (cf. O'Collins 1981:73–76)? Is the religious history of the Maasai people of Eastern Africa, both before and after the advent of Christianity among them, analogous to what the religious history of the Jewish people was for Jesus of Nazareth and still is for his followers? If the historical advent of the divine Logos presupposed the existence of a religious symbol system of communication, just as the articulation of an idea presupposes the existence of a linguistic symbol system, then the "good news" of Christianity must also presuppose the existence of many other such systems for its historically and culturally intelligible expression and celebration in different times among the world's culturally differentiated peoples.

CHRISTOLOGICAL QUESTIONS

To recognize the other religions as valid instruments of grace and meaningful expressions of faith, positively included in God's plan for the salvation of humankind, is to face an array of Christological questions that once seemed settled but currently give rise to further questions for which theologians have no neat and tidy answers. Today's catechism is a series of questions followed by more questions. How can the Galilean of nearly two thousand years ago, who was not generally recognized even by his own people as their long-expected religious leader, be recognized universally as the unique savior of the whole world and the only mediator between God and humankind?[2]

Did Jesus really see himself as the expected Messiah of the Jews? Did he identify himself as the Son of Man, later interpreted by others as the incarnate Son of God? Could the message of Jesus and the events of his life and death be understood and expressed by his followers in terms other than those available to them in their own pre-Christian religious tradition? Were the literary forms of the Bible—poetic, narrative, mythical, metaphorical—taken too literally and thus misinterpreted by early Christian writers overly influenced by the Hellenistic philosophical thought patterns and the religious symbols of their pre-Christian cultural world? Or, did these writers creatively translate the meaning of the Christ event in order to render their new faith community more intelligible to the Gentile populations of the Mediterranean basin?

The mystery of the divine presence in a particular human being would not have been shocking to pious persons in a cultural world already full of statues, indeed pantheons, of deified humans and humanized gods. The Caesars of Rome bore not only the title *pontifex maximus*, but also *divi filius* or *theou huios*, "Son of God." Even the "most Christian emperor" Justinian in the sixth century proclaimed himself sent by God to humankind as God's "personified law" (cf. Hellwig 1983:112).

Did the Greco-Roman experience, interpretation and expression of Christianity promote what Hans Küng calls an "increasingly exaggerated Christology" (Küng 1986:122–23)? The preexistence of Jesus is a theme of the Fourth Gospel (Jn 17:3–7), which reflects Hellenistic influences, but it is a theme unknown to the Synoptics and presumably foreign to the original Jewish community of Christians in Jerusalem. With the destruction of this community under Hadrian in A.D. 132 and its subsequent marginalization, even rejection, by an increasingly Hellenized ecclesiastical organization, the pristine Christology of these Jewish Christians was displaced by that of the Hellenistic Christians.

And what about the relevance today of ancient Greek metaphysics as a vehicle for expressing the meaning of what God did in Jesus of Nazareth, for example the "hypostatic union of two natures"? Is there a need for a new translation, or a reinterpretation, more suitable for populations of empiricists unaccustomed to thinking in the "third degree of abstraction"? Must the events of Easter be understood literally? Were these events more subjective than objective, metaphorically rather than literally true, results of belief rather than causes of it (cf. Lane 1975:56–65)?

DE-ABSOLUTIZING JESUS CHRIST

Christians, often with little reflection on the full meaning and the problematical implications of this belief, profess that Jesus is Christ. But this belief does not exhaust the meaning of God's interventions in human history, however conceptually or mythically or mystically or symbolically or metaphorically these might be objectified in different belief systems. "The Christ of every Christian generation," says Raimundo Panikkar, "is more than a remarkable Jewish teacher who had the fortune or misfortune of being put to death rather young" (Panikkar 1981:14). Nor is Christ an abstract principle or a disincarnate epiphany represented only by such symbols as Alpha and Omega. In the tangibility of history he signifies uniquely and climactically, according to a general belief of Christians, the proper Creator-creature relationship to which all humans are invited. "Jesus is the one," according to Jon Sobrino, "who has lived faith in all its pristine fullness, who has opened up the pathway of faith and lived it to the very end" (Sobrino 1978:107). He is, in Panikkar's words, "a living symbol for the totality of reality: human, divine and cosmic." So the question remains open whether this name "above every name" (Eph 1:21) might also be predicated of such realities as Hkambageyo,[3] or Krishna, or Purusha, or Īśvara, or even Humanity (Panikkar 1981: 27).

What we are looking for is, in the words of Gregory Baum "a way of announcing God's Word in Jesus . . . which does not devour other religions but actually makes room for the multiple manifestations of God's grace" (Baum 1975:195). In the interest of a wider ecumenism of interreligious dialogue and the obvious need to seek common ground compatible with other religious traditions, some theologians would therefore present Christianity with less emphasis upon the centrality of Jesus Christ as the unique incarnation of the divine Word and the only mediator between God and humankind. They would emphasize more the focus of Jesus himself upon the reign of God. A shift from Christocentrism to theocentrism would conform more with the preaching of Jesus; it would also provide more common ground for dialogue with the other religions. Even for Christians themselves, Christocentrism is not an end or a goal; it is a means or "way" to theocentrism (Jn 14:6).

Considering the ominous signs of the times in which we live, a soteriocentric model, with adequate attention to sacramentality and to praxis in the socioeconomic realm, might be even more appropriate.[4] Whether thematized or not, human beings all experience a need for salvation or liberation. This is why the religious symbols of salvation or liberation have, as we know from history, a latent dynamic for periodically shaking the foundations of principalities and for routing the armies of the "world rulers of this present darkness" (Eph 6:12).

When historians of religion, interpreting their findings in the light of their own Christian beliefs, point to savior figures in non-Christian religions, Christian theologians must pay careful attention. It is entirely possible, indeed very likely, that the significance for Christians of such savior figures has been hitherto overlooked because of the inevitable historico-cultural conditioning of all theology. From the standpoint of Christian doctrine, according to Karl Rahner, "there is no reason to exclude such discoveries (of extra-biblical savior figures) from the outset, or to write them off contemptuously, as if they stood in such contrast to faith in Jesus, as the eschatological and unsupersedable savior, that they can only be judged negatively" (*TI* 17:50).

In seeking answers to the novel Christological questions arising from the study of religions, theologians are bound to reflect on the gospel in the light of their own particular circumstances.[5] These must differ profoundly, according to the inevitable differences of time and place. All theological reflection and any articulation of the meaning of Jesus Christ must be done through systems of communication that are both available and intelligible to the persons concerned. They are necessarily limited not only to the locally understood languages, thought patterns, and philosophical or mythological presuppositions, but also to the local religious symbol systems which, like languages, philosophies and mythologies, are essentially ways of communicating, ways that are culturally created and historically conditioned. New Christologies, offering different emphases, formulations or interpretations, cannot therefore pretend to be universally intelligible and appropriate for all time (cf. Hellwig 1983:70–72).

Every Christology is local and ephemeral. But each is valid for its own historico-cultural situation, provided it respects the traditional, although culture-specific, parameters of classical Christology (Nicea and Chalcedon) and the normative Christologies of the New Testament. Any particular Christology is varified to the extent of its being able to manifest relatively a meaning that the eyes of faith perceive as absolutely true. This is the case with all the central symbols of Christianity, as also with the historical events that gave rise to them. These symbols "represent a particularization of the absolute," says Langdon Gilkey, "yet (they) are relative, and so only one manifestation" (Gilkey 1987:49). In Gilkey's paradox the particular symbol, culturally limited and historically conditioned, participates relatively in the absolute truth it strives to manifest representatively.

Whatever theologians may say about the "way" presented by Jesus and recorded in the New Testament, the faith of his followers expressed itself historically and culturally in a religious system of beliefs and rites and practices so focused on Jesus Christ that it came to be known as Christianity. The central and dynamic belief, always present at least residually, is that the union of the man Jesus with God is uniquely intimate and universally significant for the salvation of all human beings considered both individually and collectively. Grounded in the Jesus event of concrete human history, the incarnation, ministry, cross and resurrection are Christianity's primal and paradigmatic symbols disclosing, contrary to first appearances, the astonishingly "good news" of God's maximal participation in our human condition and destiny. Without this set of communicable beliefs and their corollaries (for example, the events of Pentecost and the final coming of Christ), whether expressed as literal or metaphorical or mythical or mystical truth, Christians would not have much more than ethical maxims and parables to contribute to an interreligious dialogue.

Here, just in passing, we may recall the narrative and mythical character of religious speaking and language. The telling of a meaningful religious story needs no special proof of its truthfulness beyond the context of its own oral or written tradition. "Myth neither requires nor includes any possible verification outside of itself," says Hans-Georg Gadamer (1980:92).

It is recognized, of course, that stories about the incarnation of the divine Logos, the ministry, death and resurrection of Jesus as the Christ, have verifiable content. However, the real importance of truth claims is in their reference not to facts in the stories as told, but to the meanings conveyed by these stories within and through the Christian faith community concerning human destiny, our self-understanding, expectations, hopes and fears.

Until a more adequate articulation is found, we must therefore continue to speak of the incarnation of the divine Word in Jesus of Nazareth, whom we believe, not without some unbelief, to be humankind's unique savior and mediator with God, while also remaining one of us. However problematical the historical and cultural particularizations of Christianity may appear at the initial stages of the interreligious dialogue in the halls of Western academia, and in spite of the inadequacies of our traditional terminology, there really is hope for a meaningful dialogue of religions.

The fact that Christians do not, in the interest of interreligious dialogue, shy away from the difficulties associated with their own central symbols is itself an indication of their honest desire for authentic dialogue. The fact that a belief is firmly held by participants in the dialogue, and held to be universally significant for the salvation of everyone, need not be interpreted as some kind of religious imperialism. To discuss one's firmly held beliefs with non-believers is not the same thing as trying to impose such beliefs upon them.

Far from trying to soften hard questions, the best hope at present for a wider ecumenism may be in a deeper understanding of the meaning of the Christian belief in the incarnation. By taking this symbol much more seriously than ever before and attempting to apply its implications to our practical relations with the members of the other faith communities, a new wisdom may eventually manifest itself in more satisfactory Christological theories and formulations, perhaps even enlightened and enriched by contributions from the other faith communities.

There is much to be learned from others. Participants in the ecumenical movement, at whatever level, know that the depths and riches of their own traditions are more fully disclosed when reconsidered in the light of other traditions.

INCARNATION AS PARADIGM

Christology determines ecclesiology. So, whether the Christ event is viewed "from above" or "from below," in the light of this or that scholarly approach, questions about the identity and mission of Jesus (his action in history) raise question about the mission of Christians in the world. If Jesus is believed to be, according to one theory or another, the incarnate Word of God and at the same time a genuine human being recognized as the risen Lord of history, then what does this say about the mission of the church as the socially and historically and culturally tangible re-presentation of Christ in and through the religious symbolism of his faith community? More precisely, what does it say about the mission of Jesus Christ that has, as its instrument in history, a religion or faith community, that is, the church that is called to become a fully catholic sign of humankind's unity and intimate union with God? And what are the methodological implications of this central belief of the Christian faith community?

To what extent is the historical mission of the incarnate Word paradigmatic for the mission entrusted by the risen Lord to his followers? Whether they understand the incarnation and the resurrection literally or metaphorically, the question is relevant to the meaning and purpose of the church. To what extent have Christians been obedient to the incarnational model in their approaches to the other religions? How extensively is this paradigm reflected today in the life of the church? How can the community of Christian believers, expressing themselves almost entirely in the terms of Jewish and European religious symbol systems, be recognized by all the others as a salutary sign raised up among the tribes and tongues and peoples and nations, inviting all who have not yet believed?

If the original faith community from which Christianity emerged is more than a mere preparation for Christianity; if the new Israel of Christianity's traditional self-understanding does not simply supersede the old Israel, but must now be understood more eschatologically in relation to the enduring significance of Judaism; then what about all the other religions? Do they parallel Christianity as the religion of Israel does? Do the other religions, like that of the Old Testament, have much to teach Christians? Does Christianity need them in the way that it needed the religion of Israel? Is the traditional belief system of a people, like their own language, a normal means of their receiving and responding humanly to God's self-communication? Are these religions the most appropriate, perhaps indispensable, instruments for a people's expression and celebration of their faith (cf. Knitter 1985:131, 149–63)? Must the Word of God, represented in the church as the universal sacrament of Christ for humankind's unity and salvation, be fully enfleshed in the cultural world of each people, through their respective pre-Christian religious symbol systems, in a manner analogous to the incarnation of the divine Word initially in Jewish cultural terms and subsequently in Greco-Roman-Iberian-Gallic-Celtic-Teutonic-Anglo-Saxon terms (more or less homogenized, in the course of centuries, as Western Christianity)?

Does the Christian faith community, for the accomplishment of its mission and for its own catholic fulfillment, need all the other religions even more than they may need Christianity?

SYNCRETISM

Even before any official interreligious dialogue is initiated, and certainly before any serious efforts are made to incarnate Christianity in the cultural worlds of non-Western peoples, the chronic ethnocentrism of the classicist mentality is apt to assert itself in the form of ominous and inhibiting admonitions against the danger of contaminating the Christian faith community with foreign and pagan elements. Must syncretic assimilations always be judged pejoratively? Is religious syncretism (that is, a confluence of different cultural elements) perhaps more often than not both desirable and necessary for the progressive universalization and tangible catholicization of Christianity?

The Old Testament's depiction of God is certainly made up of diverse cultural elements expressing varied historical perceptions of the divinity in relation to humankind. What is presented as the God of Israel has come from at least three or four different streams of tradition, and these historico-cultural sources may be further differentiated within themselves. So, what is available to us as an expression of divine revelation arose through what Wolfhart Pannenberg calls "a fusion of originally heterogeneous elements" (Pannenberg 1971:86).

Christianity, no doubt because of its missionary dynamic and incarnational model, offers a more dramatic example of religious syncretism. "This religion," writes Pannenberg, "not only linked itself to Greek philosophy, but also inherited the entire religious tradition of the Mediterranean world—a process whose details have still not been sufficiently clarified, but which was probably decisive for the persuasive power of Christianity in the ancient world" (Pannenberg 1971:87). Here we are reminded that in the classical theology of Christendom such ideas as epiphanies, mystery-type conceptualizations of the sacraments, platonized doctrines of God and grace, as well as various norms and notions borrowed from Stoicism, have become fundamental cultural symbols for the Western understanding and articulation of Judeo-Christian revelation.

The position of the Western church (or the church of the North) on syncretic assimilations by Christian communities in the non-Western world (the South) even today is determined, in actual practice, more by ethnocentrism than by theology; it reflects that of the former European colonial powers in the face of the "strange customs" and "odd concepts" of their "native" populations. Some of these assimilations are considered tolerable, even quaintly appropriate, provided they pose no threat to the church's Western cultural hegemony, or as long as it remains perfectly clear just who decides what, and how much, is to be tolerated (cf. Driver 1987:207).

DIALOGUE NEEDED

Individuals, in their encounters with others, learn who they themselves are. So also, in interreligious dialogue, separate religious groups can reach not only a greater appreciation of one another, but also a deeper understanding of what they themselves really believe. Humans, as essentially social beings, are creatures of dialogue, always in need of one another's different perspectives and surprising questions. Through conversation we grow emotionally and intellectually. One who does not listen to others is marked in every society as idiosyncratic in the pejorative sense of the term.

Dialogue "throws us into the arms of one another," says Raimundo Panikkar; it demands both trust and risk from its participants standing on an equal footing of mutual respect and attentiveness. "Dialogue," Panikkar continues, "is not simply a device for discussing or clarifying opinions, but is itself a religious category . . . a religious act, an act of faith (which comes from hearing), a mutual recognition of our human condition and its constitutive relativity." Through the diverse viewpoints and unexpected queries of others we confront the limitations of our own presuppositions, principles and horizons; we are thus invited to open ourselves to new learning and deeper understanding. "The unthought can be disclosed only by one who does not 'think' like me and who helps me discover the unthought magma out of which my thinking crystallizes" (Panikkar 1979:333). Such a service is rendered both to and by all who participate honestly in dialogue.

With good reason, if rather late in the history of Christianity, the need for interreligious "dialogue and collaboration" was officially recognized, and indeed mandated for Roman Catholics by the Second Vatican Council (cf. *NA* 2).

STRUCTURE AND LOCUS OF DIALOGUE

Both the structure and locus of interreligious dialogue must inevitably be determined by the participants themselves, as they are, within the historico-cultural contexts of their particular religious experiences and ways of understanding. The path of dialogue demonstrated by a group of German university professors of theology and the history of religion could hardly be taken as a widely applicable model. Hans Küng, Josef van Ess, Heinrich von Stietencron and Heinz Bechert, whose dialogue is recorded in their formidable volume *Christianity and the World Religions*, surely know more about the religions they discuss than do most of the ordinary believers in their respective faith communities. A study of their book would be a useful exercise for anyone preparing for formal interreligious dialogue. It should be obvious, however, that Western universities are not the most likely sites for the dialogue. The Muslims, Buddhists, Hindus, Christians, and so on usually found in these universities are not, however knowledgeable and pious they may be, typical representatives of their own traditional faith communities.

The more likely setting for fruitful dialogue would be within the cultural worlds of the people with whom Christians are now supposed to seek dialogue. This suggests immediately a new role for Christian missionaries in the non-Western world and a new outlook for the existing Christian communities in Africa, Asia and wherever else non-Christian populations are still living according to their own cultural traditions. The most meaningful interreligious encounters are apt to occur where the various traditional religions are most firmly rooted and thoroughly alive.

Missionaries, after radically reexamining their theology of evangelization in the light of Vatican II, looking thoughtfully at the contemporary world scene and the emerging theology of religions encouraged by the Council, will see an urgent need to reform drastically their strategies and methods if they are going to respond competently to the newly discovered dimensions of their ministry among the nations. And Christian communities everywhere will also have to make far-reaching changes in their attitudes and approaches to the non-Christians among whom they live. More will be said about these changes in the final chapter of this book.

THE CONTENT OF DIALOGUE

From the viewpoint of ordinary Christian believers the meaning of the "good news" announced by Jesus Christ might be the most direct and normal starting point for discussing the meaning of Christianity. Alternatively, in humble deference to the others, it might seem appropriate to listen first to what the others may have to say on a variety of topics of mutual interest. In any case the participants left to themselves are apt to choose for discussion topics of central importance to their respective faith communities.

In speaking with the followers of the traditional Maasai religion in eastern Africa, for example, a topic of great interest would be the victory over death signified by the Christian belief in the resurrection of Jesus. The Maasai people have a very weak sense of anything like life after death. For them, life is so definitively terminated at death, and the grief caused by this event is so overwhelming, that they do not like to speak of death at all. Even the names of the deceased are carefully avoided in conversations lest their mention conjure up the sadness caused by their absence. The resurrection story is so novel and intriguing to the Maasai people, touching some of them so deeply, that it might be taken as the most obvious "good news" Christians have to contribute to a religious dialogue with them. This is not the case, however, with Bantu peoples who have already a strong traditional sense of life after death. If they are followers of Islam they might prefer to start with a discussion of what they perceive to be the idolatrous polytheism of Christians.

Others, more anxious about the precarious socioeconomic plight of humankind's vast majority, or about the present potential for the total annihilation of the human species, and less attentive to cultural or religious differences as such, would argue today that the meaning of Christianity should be presented more concretely and measurably in terms of the ethical teachings of Jesus. Speaking of the last judgment story in Matthew's gospel (25:31–46), Pope John Paul II says in *Redemptor Hominis* that "this eschatological scene must always be 'applied' to humankind's history; it must always be made the 'measure' for human acts" (*RH* no. 16). Here the pope deals insistently and emphatically with "the real, 'concrete,' 'historical' human being . . . in the full truth of his (or her) existence, community and social being," while focusing on Christ's identification with the victims of sinful social structures in the modern world (ibid. nos. 13, 14).

This identification—what Jesus said about himself and "the least of these," his brothers and sisters (Mt 25:40)—discloses the most radical and disturbing meaning conveyed by the traditional incarnation symbol. In the judgment of Karl Rahner, "there is no conceivable claim which could be more radical than this, that he himself (the Lord) is always and in all cases involved in the ultimate relationship between two individuals" (*TI* 11:204). It is in people, especially the most disadvantaged and powerless, that we meet Jesus through whom we find God who is never far from any of us. In the words of Dermot Lane, "the centre of our encounter with God is our brother and our sister with whom God has united himself" (Lane 1975:141). There is no separation, in practice, between love of God and love of neighbor.

For Christians who grasp this profoundly social meaning of the incarnation, the most urgent point of departure for the wider ecumenism today might well be the ethical commonalities found in all faith communities. All religions, in ways learned through experience and enlightened by grace, however variously expressed and emphasized in different times and places, are unavoidably concerned with justice and peace. In this regard *Nostra Aetate* makes a challenging point. Through the mutual understanding to be achieved by means of dialogue, Christians and Muslims might "join in the common cause of safeguarding and fostering social justice, moral values, peace and freedom" (*NA* 3). The emphasis, at least for Christians, would then be more upon praxis than ideas, more on building a just society than speculating about the vast unknown.

Does orthopraxis, after all, determine orthodoxy? Christian living is supposed to involve action aimed at changing things for the better in the real world. Is this done primarily by correctly understanding the traditional formulations of Christian belief or through consoling rituals properly performed in aesthetically pleasing surroundings? Is growth in holiness dependent upon "head-trips" in comfortable houses of retreat from the mundane miseries and anxieties of life? Or is it primarily a matter of caring for orphans and widows, feeding the hungry, clothing the naked, sheltering the homeless, welcoming the foreigner, giving sight to the blind, liberating the captives?

Far from exempting us from theological reflection, a praxis based on what the Catholic bishops of the Americas call "a preferential option for the poor" should provoke us to further theological inquiry and interpretation. What we are doing or not doing about the plight of orphans and widows worldwide is a worthy topic for interreligious dialogue. In the specific terms of Arnulf Camps, for example, we might discuss with the followers of Islam questions such as whether the fatalism of popular Islam, or the feeling that persons are crushed by divine omnipotence and blind obedience to theocrats, "really have anything to do with authentic Islam." Then we might go on to consider whether or to what extent popular Catholicism in Latin America promotes the liberation proclaimed by Jesus or merely inclines people to resign themselves to the oppressive situations in which they find themselves while waiting for a better life in the hereafter (cf. Camps 1983:7–8, 128–31). After that we might even be ready, with the help of the others, to look critically at what passes for the Christian "way" in the Western world.

A BIBLICAL FRAME OF REFERENCE

As a way of placing the foregoing reflections within a biblical frame of reference, we may recall God's pluriform covenant relationships with humankind. The covenant made with Noah in behalf of "every living creature on earth" is universal, cosmic and everlasting, with the rainbow as its pledge visible to human beings of all times and places (Gn 9:8–17). On account of the obedience of one person to his mission, salvation is offered to all (Gn 6:18–22). There is, therefore, a general history of salvation coextensive with the history of humanity. This ecumenical alliance, embracing all the faith-communities of *homo religiosus*, is theologically as well as chronologically prior to the subsequent covenants mentioned in the Bible; it is not invalidated or superseded by them.

The covenant made with Abraham on behalf of a particular group of human beings chosen for a special mission in history, and bearing in their flesh the visible sign of the alliance, leads to a new covenant with chosen witnesses. The pledge in this case is the death and resurrection of one human being standing for all; the mission is the proclamation of this "good news" to the very ends of the inhabited earth. A part of humanity is chosen to stand for the whole and is given a mission for the sake of all. "Election is always at bottom election for others," says Joseph Ratzinger, and "election is identical with the missionary obligation" (Ratzinger 1966:80; cf. Senior and Stuhlmueller 1984: chap. 4).

The missions of the old and the new Israel constitute the special salvation history recorded as the biblical testaments. Ultimately these covenanted missions relate to "every living creature on earth," as the meaning of general and special salvation history is gradually revealed through their convergence in the course of time, with their final culmination expected in the eschatological realization of God's ecumenical purpose for all flesh. Through faithful obedience to their missions human beings progressively bring together and disclose the meaning of biblical protology and eschatology.

The real inner convergence of general and special salvation history occurs in the incipient reconciliation of all things through the hidden operations of the grace of Christ in whom the promise to Abraham is actually being fulfilled always and everywhere among persons responding, whether implicitly or explicitly, to the same saving grace that is healing, restoring, reconciling all things—although this re-creation is visible only to the eyes of faith. But the promise of blessings among the families of nations (cf. Gn 12:13) is outwardly symbolized in the tangible, consecutive and ephemeral terms of history's gradual unfolding; it is symbolized progressively, if often ambivalently and ambiguously, by the living witness of the Christian faith community among the nations, and only to the extent that this witness authentically reflects the life and death of Jesus in the real world.

This understanding of the Christian mission does not preclude the validity of other forms of witness given by other faith communities who, with Jews and Christians, have the same superabundant opportunities for responding to the same saving grace, however described in their respective belief systems. All, finally, are participants in the same judgment scene described starkly in Matthew's twenty-fifth chapter. This, when all is said and done, is decisive for all faith communities and for the destiny of each individual human being.

The universally salutary covenant of general salvation history is valid for everyone; it is superseded only among those who are actually chosen to experience special salvation history as Jews or as Christians. Like the old Israel, the new messianic people is a "little flock" in relation to all the others; "it does not actually include all people" (*LG* 9). So, as Heinz Robert Schlette points out, membership in the Christian faith community "does not consist of a more advantageous chance of salvation" (Schlette 1966:93).

Theologically (not chronologically) Christians stand with the whole of humanity on the plane of general salvation history, which is the history of humankind in the present supernatural order of existence. By and through our particular historical circumstances, however, we were called to experience faith as Christians, "not because we were or would be better than the rest of people, or so that we might attain salvation more easily; but solely because it pleased God to reveal his glory and at the same time the mystery of history, by the incomparable way of special sacred history; and because in this the lot of divine choice fell on us, in Christians terms, because God can act as seems good to him" (Schlette 1966:90). This is the mystery of election partially disclosed in the parable of the vineyard workers (Mt 20:1–6). The ecumenical implications of election for the sake of mission will be explored in the following chapter, with special attention to the significance of every religion for the catholicization of Christianity.

4

Evangelization and Dialogue in Tension

There is an obvious tension, sometimes even a blatant opposition, between the evangelical world mission of Christianity and the interreligious dialogue described in the previous chapter. Too often in the course of history the church's missionary activity has been seen merely as a device for recruiting new members. Conversion has not always been understood in the primary biblical sense of inner *metanoia* yielding a new consciousness and orientation of life in response to grace; often it has been reduced to the practice of persuading people, sometimes manipulating or even coercing them, to abandon their native religions in favor of one or another Western version of Christianity (cf. Folkemer 1976:436–38). The history of the expansion of Christianity is replete with examples of evangelization having degenerated into proselytism, an activity firmly condemned by Jesus (cf. Mt 23:15).

Is this polarity of mission and dialogue, although historically and sociologically real, merely apparent theologically? Is it inevitable? Can it be avoided? Should it be?

Some would argue today, in the light of observations made in the foregoing pages, that the tension or opposition between interreligious dialogue and the evangelizing mission of Christianity can be reduced only if the church moderates its anxious zeal for numerical growth among non-Christian peoples and curtails its officially organized missionary outreach. This final chapter argues, in contrast, that the opposition between evangelization and dialogue is not inevitable; it can and should be excluded. The tension may indeed remain, but it can and should be mutually creative.

MISSION MISCONCEIVED

As elements of particular cultures, faith communities throughout the world suffer, some more acutely than others, from a universal human inclination to identify their own culturally formed and historically conditioned fragments of knowledge and creativity with divine omniscience and omnipotence, thereby positioning themselves for the enactment of untold mischief in the name of God (cf. Gn 3:6). No faith community is immune to humankind's congenital and chronic ethnocentrism with its concomitant arrogance. Nor is any religious system free from the temptations of power with its associated pathologies, whether these are expressed in subtle gestures or in copious bloodletting. Ethnocentric posturing in the religious realm, especially when associated with the exercise of power over alien peoples, has a long and painful history. These malign forces, more than any single theological issue, are major obstacles to interreligious understanding and harmonious interaction.

The Creator's work is gloriously and invincibly pluriform. The diverse cultural creations of humanity, made in God's image, are necessarily varied and variable. Against this irreducible cultural pluriformity Christians have striven for centuries not just to evangelize others, but to impose upon them the fragile religious forms and ephemeral social structures invented or accumulated during the formative stages of Western cultural history. There is a tacit assumption that all of humankind, originally made in the image of God, must be remade in the Western image, as though people would be pleasing to God to the extent that they approximate the ways of Western Christians. This confusing of evangelization with the imposition of particular cultural forms, structures, articulations and celebrations of belief certainly smacks of idolatry; it turns "good news" immediately into bad news. Then the whole meaning of Christianity's central symbol, the incarnation of the divine Word in Jesus of Nazareth, is missed.

This is why Karl Rahner could critically liken the church's actual missionary activity to "that of an export firm, exporting to the whole world a European religion along with other elements of this supposedly superior culture and civilization, and not really attempting to change the commodity" (*TI* 20:78). As causative factors behind this arrogance Rahner points to the higher levels of Roman Catholic officialdom, although his remarks might apply equally, *mutatis mutandis*, to many other mission-sending agencies, Protestant as well as Catholic:

Have not the Roman Congregations always had the mentality of a centralized bureaucracy, claiming to know what is best everywhere in the world for the service of the Kingdom of God and the salvation of souls, and do not their decisions appear to be shockingly naive, based as they are on the assumption that the Roman or Italian mentality is the obvious standard of judgment? (*TI* 20:79).

Thus the church, rigidly identified with only a European experience and expression of Christianity, and in contradiction to its own catholic nature,

sought to establish itself as such in the rest of the world without the risk of a really new beginning, breaking with some of the continuities which had been taken for granted, as was shown in the various rites controversies, in the export of the Latin liturgical language into countries where Latin had never been an historical factor, in the way in which Roman law was exported as a matter of course in Canon Law, in the naive way in which it was taken for granted that the bourgeois morality of the West could be imposed in every detail on people of alien cultures, in the rejection of religious experiences of other cultures, etc. (*TI* 20:86).

This is why Christian communities outside of Europe and North America generally resemble nothing so much as Western spiritual colonies. "A Christianity of empire," says the African theologian Eboussi Boulaga, "imposes itself only by tearing up its converts by the roots, out of where-they-live, out of their being-in-the-world, presenting them with the faith only at the price of depriving them of their capacity to generate the material and spiritual conditions of their existence" (Boulaga 1984:17). In contrast to this alien religion of imported forms, structures, rules, conceptions and abstractions, Boulaga speaks poignantly of the African religious experience that was scorned when not simply ignored by missionaries: "It was being born, living, and dying, in the most empirical manner that ever could be, that furnished the framework, the matter, and the experience of God's sacramentality and sovereign immanence" (ibid:27).

The prepackaged Christianity still being propagated among non-Western peoples, although now embellished with a few tokens borrowed from indigenous traditions, is manifestly that of Western bourgeois society with all of its inherent fetishes, notably its excessive and dis-integrating individualism and utilitarianism. As in the West, this leads eventually to "post Christianity," after which there is no religion at all. As in the West also, in spite of everything, a faithful remnant remains, because God's grace is greater than humankind's obtuseness. But there are increasing numbers of believing Christians who do not "practice the faith" in these foreign ways, just as there are increasing numbers who still "practice" while no longer believing.

The gospel call to repentance does not require the repudiation of any authentic cultural heritage. Only sin is repudiated. People need the integrity of their respective cultures not only for their humanization but also for their divinization (cf. Best 1977:250). God's Word is spoken to them naturally and normally in their own concrete historical experience and cultural terms, not in the terms of some other people's history and culture. Although all cultures, like all the children of Adam (after as well as before baptism) are flawed, it is God who allotted to all tribes and peoples and nations their respective times and places; he is not far from any of them (cf. Acts 10:35, 45; 11:12, 17; 15:22–28). Even as the Holy Spirit is able to speak to persons in any human context, so also the gospel is capable of functioning as a transforming l aven in every society (cf. Paul VI *EN*:20). Meanwhile, according to ancient Christian belief, the world awaits the advent of God's Word in Jesus Christ, who does not break the bruised reed nor quench the smoldering wick in any existing faith community. An incarnational missionary approach, as we know from the life and death of Jesus, accepts the religious experience of, and enters into crucial dialogue with, the people to whom the missionary is sent. Does the church that calls itself "essentially missionary" accept and enter into dialogue with the religio-cultural worlds of those for whom the Christian faith community exists, namely, all the peoples of the world to whom the church is sent and from whom the church is called forth (cf. *AG* 22)? Does the church's official missionary practice positively encourage these diverse peoples to understand and express the meaning of Christianity in the culture-specific and historically conditioned terms of their respective and vastly differentiated social, economic, artistic and religious experiences?

It is only in this incarnational way that people are enabled "to bring forth from their own living traditions original expressions of Christian life, celebration and thought," as Pope John Paul II said in *Catechesi Tradendae* (1979 no. 53). These "original expressions" are what Cardinal Otunga of Nairobi, Kenya, called "flowers that have never been seen before" in the church (Otunga 1978:28). But where are they? When will we see them in bloom throughout the non-Western world? Only when those engaged in the missionary and pastoral ministries begin to take more seriously the practical implications of their belief in the incarnation of the divine Word.

INCARNATION MISCONSTRUED

There is a popular tendency among Christians to conceptualize Jesus Christ in terms of the divinity, without taking adequate account of his humanity and its implications for the life of the church (cf. Murphy-O'Connor 1978:33–78; Congar 1957 *passim*). "A strange and unconscious line of thought all too often and too easily asserts itself," says Karl Rahner, "by which Jesus comes simply to be identified with God" (*TI* 4:105–20; 11:194–99). This is especially manifest in devotional attitudes and practices. In the words of Cardinal Joseph Ratzinger:

> The truth of the humanity of Christ got left more and more in the shade in the course of the centuries, and in practice Jesus was seen only as God. So there occurred something like a concealment or a clear Monophysitism in Christian piety (Ratzinger 1981:153).

Consequently, "Christian consciousness has not yet been sufficiently activated in all its amplitude" by a practical belief in the true humanity of Jesus (ibid.). Among Roman Catholics this monophysite tendency has been too readily carried over into ecclesiology, ascribing to the ecclesiastical institution attributes appropriate only to the divinity, thus allowing official servants of the church sometimes to act as though the fallen condition of humanity were not integral to the nature of the institutional church and not reflected in its official conduct (cf. Congar 1957:60–62).

So there are good reasons for repeating once again that Jesus of Nazareth is not a disguise used by God, not a human outer garment covering the divinity, not something extrinsic to what we are. In him the divine Word became one of us, like ourselves in our everyday experience of life, circumscribed by the events of one gradually unfolding historical period, constrained by the particularity of time, place, ethnicity and culture, while thinking, acting and loving with a human mind, will and heart (cf. Rahner *SM* 3:110–18; *TI* 4:105–20; 11:194–99; *FC*:195–228).

The Christian understanding of the relationship between God and humankind is dominated by a belief in the incarnation of the divine Word.[1] This belief, however problematical it has always been for theologians, requires us to take seriously the meaning of finitude, flesh, history and culture. God so loves the world that he assumes human nature from the inside, thus giving himself over to a mode of existence not his previously. Whatever this may mean to Greek metaphysicians, it surely symbolizes to believing Christians some kind of divine self-donation (self-bestowal or self-communication) through which humanity is intimately embraced from within. It also involves an incomprehensible self-emptying. In giving himself (herself or itself, we know not which) to humankind in this radical manner, the divine Logos discounted his divinity and "humbled himself" to become truly one of us (cf. Phil 2:6–8): like ourselves in "a body of flesh" (Col 1:22), "born of a woman" (Gal 4:4), "descended from" a particular family, clan and tribe in a distinctive ethnic-culture group "according to the flesh" (Rom 1:3).

THE PRINCIPLE OF INCARNATION

What God has done in Jesus is paradigmatic for the faith community of Christians in their mandatory outreach to the whole of humankind: "As the Father has sent me, even so I send you" (Jn 20:21). This missionary ministry to the ends of the earth, hence the nature of the church, is derived directly from, and supposedly modeled upon, the scandalous belief that the divine Logos became authentically one of us in *everything* except sin (cf. Heb 2:14–18; 4:15). The church, as a culturally enfleshed sociological reality within tangible human history, is still far from its eschatological perfection (*LG* 48; *GS* 43). Like Jesus, the Christian faith community also suffers the constraints of the human condition, but with the added burden of being peccable. The church is a holy community of sinners always in need of repentance, enlightenment and purification (*LG* 8).

The Second Vatican Council, in spite of all appearances to the contrary, reaffirmed the ancient Christian teaching that "the Church, sent to all peoples of every time and place, is not bound exclusively and indissolubly to any race or nation, nor to any particular way of life or any customary pattern of living, ancient or recent" (*GS* 58). Instead, the church is expected to grow in catholicity and to become progressively a world church while at the same time being at home in the particular cultural world of each people. The mission is to be accomplished by the church entering "into communion with varied forms of culture, thereby enriching both itself and the cultures themselves" (ibid.).

Missionary activity, therefore, is never supposed to be a matter of displacing the religio-cultural experiences of non-Christian peoples and replacing them with the Western world's historically developed and culturally articulated experience of Christian revelation. Rather, the missionary ministry is supposed to entail "a wonderful exchange, in keeping with the economy of the incarnation—*ad instar oeconomiae incarnationis*" (*AG* 22). The church's missionary task, as understood by Karl Rahner, is one of "making Christ, his gospel and his grace present among all peoples as such in their own specific histories and cultures, and thereby of achieving a quite new incarnational presence of Christ himself in the world" (*TI* 12:176). But this cannot be done where the principle of incarnation (inculturation) is ignored (cf. Hillman 1987:510–13).

In this way all the cultural riches of the nations are assumed by Christ who is significantly present in his believing community (as the sacrament of Christ) in the physical, historical and cultural flesh of humankind's tribes and tongues and peoples (*AG* 22). Thus the Christian faith community in its ecclesial structure, if it is ever to become a universally intelligible sign of humankind's unity and salvation, "*must* implant itself among these groups—the large and distinct groups united by enduring ties, ancient religious traditions, and strong social relationships—*in the same way* that Christ by his *incarnation* committed himself to the *particular social and cultural circumstances* of the people among whom he lived" (*AG* 10, italics added).

It was a profound understanding of the ecclesial implications of the mystery of the incarnation that prompted the Jesuit Superior General, Pedro Arrupe, to speak out boldly on the issue of the church's parsimonious cultural pluralism (or its European monocultural mania), an issue raised by bishops from Africa, India and parts of Asia during the 1977 synod of bishops in Rome. Against those discomforted by proposals encouraging historically new and culturally different expressions and celebrations of Christian belief and life; against those who feared that non-Western ways of being human and Christian might possibly contradict what we (Europeans) have formulated and put into practice up to now, Arrupe argued that "real pluralism is the most profound unity," and that the present "crisis, in many cases, is due to insufficient pluralism which fails to provide the satisfaction of expressing and living one's faith in conformity with one's own culture" (Arrupe 1978:21).

Although somewhat obliquely, in a rhetorical question referring specifically to Africa, Pope Paul VI had already acknowledged this "insufficient pluralism." In a 1975 address to six cardinals and forty bishops from Africa and Madagascar he touched upon the issue with this question: "Does the Church in Africa retain a certain Christian religious form that was brought from outside and which makes her, as it were, a stranger and pilgrim among her peoples?" (*EA*:294). This very question had already been answered unambiguously, although with his usual caution, by the same pope during an earlier visit to Africa:

A certain pluralism is not only legitimate but also desirable. An adaptation of the Christian life in the fields of pastoral, ritual, didactic and spiritual activities is not only possible, it is even favored by the Church. . . . And in this sense, you may and you must, have an Africa Christianity (*DA* 1969:48–51).

Pope John Paul II, commenting on St. Paul's positive missionary approach to, and his accepting attitude toward, cultures other than his own, noted regretfully that "in practice there has not always been full correspondence with this high ideal" (*RH* 12). Such reticence in criticizing the church's practical identification of the Christian "way" with Western ways of being Christian recalls what may well be the greatest understatement of the Second Vatican Council: "Experience shows that, because of circumstances, it is sometimes difficult to harmonize culture with Christian teaching" (*GS* 62).

The bishops of Africa and Asia have been much less reserved. In their report to the 1974 synod of bishops in Rome the episcopal representatives from eastern Africa spoke vigorously of the need for much more cultural pluralism in the life of the church among the nations. "It is necessary," they argued, "to foster the particular incarnation of Christianity in each country, in accordance with the genius and the talents of each culture, so that 'a thousand flowers may bloom in God's garden.'" In their final statement at the synod the African bishops returned again to this major concern of theirs that the Christian life was "insufficiently incarnated into African ways, customs and traditions," and that it was "very often lived merely at the surface without any real link or continuity with the genuine values of traditional religions" (African Bishops 1975:43, 56, 58). The Asian bishops were equally outspoken in their report to the 1977 synod in Rome: "As God became one of us—to make us his own—his church in Asia must be Asian, like the Asians in all things, except sin" (quoted in McGregor 1977:65).

In spite of all the official directives and the eloquent lip service given to the principle of incarnation (or inculturation), church officials worldwide still cling generally to the European model of Christian life and church structure developed during the centuries of European imperialism. The persistent paternalism found in this model is now expressed more guardedly, but it is still firmly in control even where some token recognition of local ways of being human and religious have been permitted. So the general image of the church outside of Europe and North America still remains overwhelmingly alien in its institutions, rules, concepts, rites and practices, including in some Catholic parishes imported statues of lifelike painted plaster which are more reminiscent of Mediterranean polytheism than of the New Testament. Presented in the dazzling garb of foreign wealth and power, Christianity still appears as a superior folk religion trying to displace the traditional religions of peoples considered "undeveloped." Such a climate is hardly congenial to the idea of an authentically incarnational and evangelical dialogue.

THE CHURCH AS MISSION

What God has done in Jesus Christ "once and for all" (Heb 7:27; 9:26–28) in the historico-cultural terms of one particular people, the church must do in sacramentality among all the peoples who, with their varied historical experiences, myriad cultures and social structures, constitute the whole of humanity in its spacio-temporal reality. After the manner of the divine Logos the church must go out of herself, emptying herself of power, foreign riches and alien accretions, thus opening herself to modes of human existence, experience, expression and celebration that were not previously hers.

The church, in other words, is to make herself completely at home among each people in the same authentically human way that Jesus was at home in Nazareth. To ignore the missionary implications of belief in the incarnation in relation to humankind's cultural pluriformity is to foreclose the church's real growth in genuine catholicity. This is why cultures, far from being despised or ignored by missionaries, must be evangelized, as Pope Paul VI said, "not in a purely decorative way as it were by applying a thin veneer, but in a vital way, in depth and right to their very roots, in the wide and rich sense which these terms have in *Gaudium et Spes*" (*EN* 20).

Instead of thinking of the church as having a mission to the nations, it is more helpful to think of the mission of Jesus Christ having a church as its instrument. The proper use of this instrument of mission is indicated in the symbolism of the incarnation of the divine Logos. The Christian faith-community's missionary outreach, understood in this way, is more than compatible with interreligious dialogue. It is precisely for such a dialogue on a global scale that the church, as a continuation in sacramental symbolism of the one mission of the divine Logos, is sent to the whole inhabited earth. As Christ is the sacrament of God, so the church is the sacrament of Christ for the world (cf. Rahner *TI* 14:179–81). Indeed, this is why the church exists as a part of humanity standing for the whole: to take on the physical, historical and cultural flesh of each people, thus becoming among them an indigenously intelligible witness to humankind's unity and salvation, so that all might recognize themselves and one another for what they are—God's own people.

As the community of those chosen and sent as witnesses to the ends of the earth, the church is supposed to be a tangible sign raised up among the nations inviting all to believe the "good news" that, in spite of all contrary appearances, the hidden but victorious grace of God is working always and everywhere, superabundantly, for the unity and salvation of humankind. The pledge of this, for those who believe it and are thereby enabled to carry the "good news" to the peoples who have not yet heard it "in the lands beyond" (2 Cor 10:16), is the man Jesus. In him the divine Word experiences historically actual human existence in everything save sin. In this event we learn that God is encountered primarily, if not exclusively, in the realm of human relations, indeed in human beings (cf. Jn 14:19; Mt 25:31–46). We see also that God speaks to people normally, if not exclusively, through their own culturally created and historically conditioned symbol systems. Then we begin to wonder why the peoples of the whole world should be expected to respond to God's Word and celebrate the divine presence in the culturally created and historically conditioned symbols systems of only one small segment of the human family.

So, for those who believe in him, Jesus Christ is an assurance of the unifying and saving presence of God among all peoples. The incarnation symbolizes God's self-donation to humankind in such a way that everyone, always and everywhere, is enabled by the Holy Spirit to find salvation— unless he or she ultimately, and with a bad conscience, freely rejects this offer of new and fuller life. This is "what the Christian message is all about," says Karl Rahner; this is "what Christianity really is and mediates and means." Every human being is made in God's image and called to live accordingly, as "the *event* of the free, unmerited and forgiving self-communication of God in absolute closeness and immediacy" (*FC* 116–17, 138–39). This is the "good news" on account of which all Christians are supposed to be missionaries. Such is the "mystery hidden for ages and generations," but now made manifest, concerning the greatness of God and the glory of his riches among the nations (Col 1:26–27; Eph 3:9). Thus, as Raimondo Panikkar reminds us, "the real challenge of Christian faith today comes from within, i.e., from an inner dynamic toward universality, from its own claim to 'catholicity' " (1979:325).

EVANGELICAL DIALOGUE

In his effort to align the ecclesiastical bureaucracy with the new directions mandated by the Second Vatican Council, Pope Paul VI established the Secretariat for Non-Christians as an organism distinct from the Congregation for the Evangelization of Peoples (formerly the Congregation for the Propagation of the Faith). Both of these organizational structures are concerned with, although from rather different viewpoints, the same population, namely, the vast majority of the human family who are not Christians. A cursory consideration of the two agencies, their diverse perspectives, especially in the light of previous missionary practice, suggests the existence of an antipathetic relationship between them. For Pope Paul, however, the missionary task and the Council's call for dialogue and collaboration with the followers of other religions were complementary, because real evangelization must always be, as it was in the original incarnational model, accomplished only in dialogue.

In this context dialogue is not a technique or a device for leading people along the path of conversion from one faith community to another. While the option must always be open for Christians as well as non-Christians to change their religious orientation by entering a different faith community, all forms of calculated persuasion or manipulation remain completely incompatible with the mutual freedom and respect required for honest interreligious dialogue. In this regard, Christians need to remind themselves that their own firm beliefs about Jesus Christ as the incarnate Word of God, the Lord of history and the unique savior of the whole world, are internal faith claims, based on interpretations of a historical revelation peculiar to their own community of faith. These beliefs have their counterparts, but not their equivalents, in other religious systems. So we must always beware of the "supercilious condescension" with which Christians often disregard the subjective faith claims of others, while expecting the others to appreciate the subjective faith claims of Christians (cf. Sizemore 1976:416).

On Pentecost Sunday 1964, appropriately recalling the Pentecostal events recorded in the Acts of the Apostles when persons from every nation heard God's word expressed in their respective historico-cultural terms, the new Secretariat for Non-Christians was instituted by Pope Paul VI. In the constitution *Regimini Ecclesiae*: the pope described as its purpose

to search for methods and ways of opening a suitable dialogue with non-Christians. It should strive, therefore, in order that non-Christians come to be known honestly and esteemed justly by Christians, and that in their turn non-Christians can adequately know and esteem Christian doctrine and life (quoted in Secretariat 1984 no. 4).

While creative theologians like Raimundo Panikkar and Paul Knitter continue their explorations and raise further questions about the significance of Christianity in relation to the other religions, the Secretariat for Non-Christians has directly responded to the question of the relationship between mission and dialogue. In a 1984 document called *The Attitude of the Church Towards the Followers of Other Religions: Reflections and Orientation on Dialogue and Mission*, an answer is given in terms not of either-or, but both-and. Dialogue includes mission, and mission presupposes dialogue.

Evangelization, after all, consists in sharing with the entire human family God's "good news" expressed as belief in the hopeful significance of the life and death of Jesus Christ. This sustaining belief of the Christian faith community can and should be seen as "good tidings" for the whole inhabited earth. And what is interreligious dialogue, if not essentially a mutual sharing of, and listening to, God's "good news" as experienced and expressed variously in the diverse belief systems of the different times and places in which human beings have found themselves trying to respond to a Word from the eternal? For these religions "ultimately," as Wolfhart Pannenberg says, "have to do with the same divine reality as the message of Jesus" (Pannenberg 1971:115).

Authentic dialogue, as described by the Secretariat for Non-Christians, always allows people, indeed encourages them, to be themselves: "It leaves room for the other person's identity, modes of expression and values." This, moreover, is "the norm and necessary manner of every form of Christian mission," to the extent that "any sense of mission not permeated by such a dialogical spirit would go against the demands of true humanity and against the teaching of the gospel" (Secretariat 1984 no. 29). The point was made unambiguously at the 1974 Synod in Rome by, among others, Cardinal Darmojuwono of Indonesia:

> To implant the church is to enter into dialogue with the cultures and the religions of the country. The object of this dialogue is to render gradually more explicit and conscious the presence of God's Spirit, which transforms and penetrates human beings' lives (quoted in Boff 1986:25).

This kind of mutual sharing of God's "good news" is apt to yield unexpected results in terms of enriching, modifying, correcting and developing the traditional religious beliefs of the participants, even transforming profoundly the religious consciousness of some and leading them into different paths, including the "way" indicated by the Christ event. But the process is ever free and open-ended, never an imposition of anyone's particular religious belief system upon others. Allowance must always be made, therefore, and respect maintained, for the possibility of Christians as well as others being led freely by the Spirit from one faith community to another.

Such a dialogue, courageously open to new beginnings, can be mutually enriching; it holds the promise of increasing unity and fuller life for all of humankind. From a specifically Christian viewpoint the dialogue may be understood also as evangelical. It is in no way opposed to the church's missionary ministry; rather, it is a more appropriate way for the church to be "essentially missionary" (*AG* 2, 6, 35, 36), reaching out to the ends of the earth not in some imperial posture but in response to the summons of the Holy Spirit who is already present among all peoples. The ecumenical purpose of the church, sent by Jesus Christ and moved by the Holy Spirit, is to make itself "fully present to all persons and peoples" (*AG* 5). This mission, as we know from almost two thousand years of history, is not well-served by the methods of an export firm, much less by the ways of imperial or colonial invaders and manipulators, imposing their specifically European or North American religious experiences, expressions and celebrations upon the peoples of the much larger world elsewhere.

Evangelical dialogue is a radically different method that calls for a far-reaching reform of Christianity's contemporary missionary thinking and activity. The incarnational method of evangelical dialogue, exemplified dramatically by Jesus, is a challenge presented to the whole Christian world by the teaching of Vatican II on the significance of the other faith communities. The challenge is as dangerous, and its consequences as unpredictable, as the challenge faced by the Lord Jesus whose mission the church is supposed to continue symbolically among the nations. In the words of Vatican II, "The Church, prompted by the Holy Spirit, must walk the same road which Christ walked: a road of poverty and obedience, of service and self-sacrifice to the death, from which death he came forth a victor by his resurrection" (*AG* 5). In spite of all appearance to the contrary—for example, the anxieties expressed by Jesus shortly before his murder and the sense of failure reflected in the conduct of the apostles—the final outcome of his historical mission was a joyful surprise.

A willingness to take risks, with a confident faith in the Spirit—a readiness even to face the dangers of dying in a variety of ways for the sake of a new and fuller life—is a requirement of the church's obedience to the mission entrusted to her by the risen Lord. His obedience to mission is the church's model. This mission, directed outward to the nations, even to the ends of the earth, is a call to leave behind the cultural accouterments and historical accretions of Christianity's European past. It is a call for new beginnings, for speaking in strange tongues and expressing Christ's "good news" through different religious symbols in the more numerous and vastly diverse cultural worlds of peoples living outside the walls of ancient Christendom. The church is the church, after all, only to the extent that it exists, not as a theological abstraction, but as a palpable social entity for the whole of humankind. Without this wider ecumenical vision and missionary commitment, the church retains the image of a European folk religion.

LIBERATION THEOLOGY

Christian missionary activity understood and practiced according to the incarnational model and in the form of an evangelical dialogue with the followers of other religions complements the contemporary Christian movement called liberation theology as articulated by Gregory Baum and by Gustavo Gutiérrez. Both the incarnational and the liberationist approaches call for critical theological reflection on the church's missionary and pastoral activities. This entails a prophetic task of discerning the structural consequences of these ministries as carried out in practice, then evaluating the consequences according to the norms of the gospel and the church's own formal teachings—all with a view to enabling the church "to restructure its concrete social presence so that its social consequences approach more closely its profession of faith" (Baum 1975:194–95).

Both of these evolving dimensions of theological reflection, incarnational and liberationist, find their inspiration in biblical themes and in a compassionate concern for the victims of systemic injustice on a massive scale. And both aim at the emancipation of people from situations of dependence upon, or domination by, alien forms and forces. There is also a common emphasis on God's universal salvific will as something always active in the mundane experience of peoples. Salvation is not reduced to a pious concept of individual souls privately embraced by God now and in the hereafter; it is salvation of whole persons and peoples loved in their actual human condition, historical situation and cultural matrices. For Gustavo Gutiérrez, the incarnation of the divine Word has social, political and economic implications as well as religious significance. In his words:

> The liberating action of Christ—made man in this history and not in a history marginal to the real life of man—is at the heart of the historical current of humanity; the struggle for a just society is in its own right very much a part of salvation history (Gutierrez 1973:168).

The critical focus of the incarnational missionary approach is on the injustice of peoples being denied the validity of their own indigenous cultures as ways of experiencing, understanding and expressing the meaning of their faith. "The true religion" was too often presented by missionaries almost exclusively as a matter of *imitating* the religious practices, attitudes, forms, styles and interpretations of Western peoples. In the name of God whole populations were persuaded to abandon the religious symbol systems that had nurtured their faith and sustained their cultures for countless generations. In the name of Jesus Christ they were urged to forfeit their most profoundly formative cultural elements, and then to appropriate the ways of the West in religion and, by implication, in philosophy, art, ethics, law and economics.

There is an obvious parallel with liberation theology's special focus upon the political and economic injustices perpetrated by the same Western powers through their control and manipulation, for their own benefit, first of colonial empires and now of global economic systems. "True socio-economic progress" was presented to the inhabitants of poor nations as a matter of *imitating* the processes followed earlier by the more "developed" nations of the West. This meant that for the sake of economic growth the poor must become poorer as ancient oligarchs and emerging middle-class elites, in league with interested foreign powers and corporations, became progressively richer. Development was understood as increasing material wealth, with little regard for its equitable distribution. Progress came to mean the creation of greater riches for fewer people, and greater poverty for more people.

One might wonder which injustice is more devastating or where to begin laying foundations for a just society. Which should be addressed first: the progressive disintegration of a people's cultural identity and self-understanding in relation to God and the rest of humankind, or the deprivation of a population's political power and economic opportunity? Both of these injustices are profound affronts to the essential dignity of human persons. So the incarnational and the liberationist dimension of critical theological reflection may be seen as mutually supportive. Still, the advocates of each approach need to take more seriously the other's perspective.[2]

RESOLVING THE MISSION-DIALOGUE QUESTION

Although the Second Vatican Council did not finally resolve the questions it raised concerning the relationship of the church's universal mission and the Council's call for dialogue and collaboration with the followers of the other religions, it did open the way for further theological inquiry and possible development along the lines already suggested by the contemporary theologians cited frequently in the previous pages. The writings of Pope Paul VI, already noted, on the meaning of interreligious dialogue and missionary evangelization in our culturally pluralistic world context may also be counted as significant contributions to the development of theology; they amount, moreover, to an official blessing on the radically new ways of viewing not only the other religions but also the global mission entrusted to Christians.

Had the Jesus model been followed faithfully by missionaries sent to the peoples living outside the cultural zones of Europe; had they been encouraged, or at least permitted, to approach the cultures of the other tribes and peoples and nations in the incarnational and dialogical manner attempted by Matteo Ricci in China and Roberto de Nobili in India, then surely the global garden of God would now be blooming with a thousand flowers never seen before. The church might also have become a more authentically catholic, hence more intelligible, sign of blessing among the nations and more fully at home with the followers of other religions. Yet it is not too late.

It is never too late to respond to God's will as we understand it according to the flickering lights available in our own time. We must remember, however, that the way of incarnation and dialogue will involve astonishing events and yield unexpected results, perhaps even a death and burial before a resurrection to a fuller life.

CONCLUSION

The prayer of Cardinal Nicholas of Cusa (1401–64) is an appropriate conclusion to the foregoing reflections on the wider ecumenism. If thoughtfully recited, this petition should help Christians today to prepare the way

for Christians of the future to see the dawning of a new day of Pentecost —
when church leaders will not only speak to all peoples in their respective
tongues (cf. Acts 2:4–12), but will also listen to the others as they express
in their own ways what God has been doing among them from time im-
memorial:

> It is Thou, O God, who is being sought in the various religions in
> various ways, and named with various names, for Thou remainest as
> Thou art, to all incomprehensible and inexpressible. Be gracious and
> show Thy countenance.... When Thou wilt graciously perform it,
> then the sword, jealous hatred and all evil will cease, and all will come
> to know that there is but *one* religion in the variety of religious cus-
> toms (quoted in Thompson 1976:381).

Notes

1. RELIGION: A COMPONENT OF CULTURE

1. For the Dinka myth, see Leonhardt (1973:108–12). The reference to a similar myth of the Maasai is based on my own first-hand experience among these people.

2. For more on this question, which is still debated, see Dodd (1951:25), Roman 1948:3–5, 21–22, 34–39), Milhaven (1970:37–39), Hillman (1973:264–75), Frankena (1973:295–317), Curran (1987:52–64).

3. For an elaboration of the notion of faith as a universally available free act of self acceptance implying an acceptance of God, see Karl Rahner (*TI* 16:64–67): "Whenever a person does not reject himself in a final denial, and does not utter an ultimate protest in total scepticism or despair, even though this acceptance is mediated and obscured by categorial objects of choice, then there is present what Christians call 'faith.' "

For William Cantwell Smith, "Faith is an orientation of the personality, to one-self, to one's neighbour, to the universe; a total response; a way of seeing the world and of handling it; a capacity to live at more than the mundane level; to see, to feel, to act in terms of, a transcendent dimension" (1981:113–14).

4. "One of the definitions of faith commonly given by Muslims is that faith is one's existential *engagement* with what one knows to be true or good, obligatory. It is the committing of oneself to act in terms of what one recognizes as cosmically valid" (Smith 1981:119).

2. CHRISTIAN THEOLOGY AND THE UBIQUITY OF GRACE

1. On the knowledge of Christians concerning peoples in distant lands as early as the second century, see Hans Küng et al. (1986:161–62).

2. For more on this and the theologians who, against St. Augustine and the Latin theologians, retained the earlier Greek tradition of a much broader way of salvation, see Drummond (1985: chaps. 4 and 5), Theisen (1976: passim); Burns (1976:54–75).

3. See also Rahner (*TI* 1:297–317; 4:165–88; *SM* 2:415–27).

4. See Fitzmyer (1986:90): "A Christology 'from above' (or a descent Christology) is a title for an approach that either uses the traditional explanation of Jesus Christ as the God-man (especially in its Calcedonian formulation) or uses the incarnation as a starting point. A Christology 'from below' (or an ascent Christology) begins rather with the gospel data about Jesus of Nazareth in his earthly ministry and moves to an acknowledgment of him as Lord and Son of God. Neither term is

per se negative or pejorative; it merely describes the thrust of the approach used."

5. For an elaboration and defense of this central and recurring theme of Rahner's, see Rahner (*TI* 5 chap. 6; 6 chaps. 16 and 23; 9 chap. 9; 12 chap. 17; 17 chap. 5; 18 chap. 17). For a summary, see Riesenhuber (1965:163–71). For a succinct explanation of Rahner's key ideas, see Richard (1981:29–35); also Edwards (1986:18–30). For some criticisms of, and developments beyond, Rahner's soteriology, see Schineller (1976:552–66).

6. For a systematic response to objections raised against the idea of an implicit or anonymous Christianity, see D'Costa (1985:passim).

3. TOWARD A WIDER ECUMENSIM

1. The teaching of Vatican II on revelation was "concerned with overcoming neo-scholastic intellectualism, for which revelation chiefly meant a store of mysterious supernatural teachings, which automatically reduces faith very much to an acceptance of these supernatural insights." As a corrective, "the Council desired to express again the character of revelation as . . . a true dialogue which touches man in his totality . . . addressing him as a partner . . . giving him his true nature for the first time" (Ratzinger 1969:172). According to Yves Congar, "the great weakness of scholastic theology is its lack of a historical sense. . . . The absence of this sense consists in locating everything in one's present personal context. . . . Many times (this) has pushed the medieval Masters into interpreting the terms and statements of the Bible not as a part of the Bible itself but as ideas of their time and their milieu, or again as theoretical ideas sometimes foreign to the literal and historic sense of the text. . . . Only rarely did the Middle Ages have this historic sense. It was interested in objectivity, the absolute character of the object, the equating of the intellect with a kind of knowing endowed with perfect certitude" (Congar 1968:139).

2. For an erudite survey of contemporary Christology, including a guided tour through some of its most tangled terrain, see Paul Knitter (1985:145–203; 1986:116–35). For the contemporary questions raised concerning the meaning of the incarnation, see John Hick (1980:19, 27–8, 58–9, 72–5). See also William M. Thompson (1976:381, 395–409), Peter J. Schineller (1976:545–66), Monika Hellwig (1983:passim) and Dermot Lane (1975:passim).

For the argument that the incarnation of the divine Word should be understood as metaphor, and universal Christocentric exclusivism abandoned by Christians in favor of a more ecumenical theocentrism, see John Hick (1977; 1980). See also the response of Gavin D'Costa (1984; 1986a; 1986b; 1987), who also offers insightful critiques of Knitter (1985) and Race (1983).

3. Hkambageyo is a Christ-like historical figure who is central to the traditional religion of the Batem people (also called Sonjo) of northern Tanzania.

4. See Knitter's response to the constructive comments of Denise Lardner Carmody and William Cenker (Knitter et al. 1986: 122–30, 134); also Knitter (1987:170–200).

5. For a thoughtful analysis of this notion of theology as a product of the "dynamic interaction among gospel, church and culture," see Robert J. Schreiter (1985:1–21).

4. EVANGELIZATION AND DIALOGUE IN TENSION

1. For a readable exposition of the meaning of the incarnation, see Dermot Lane (1975: chap. 9).
2. For more on this see Paul Knitter (1987:178–200).

References

African Bishops. "Report on the Experiences of the Church in the Work of Evangelization in Africa" and "Statement of the Bishops of Africa." *African Ecclesial Review* 17/1 (1975).

Aquinas, St. Thomas. *Summa Theologica*. Trans. English Dominicans. New York: Benziger, 1947.

———. *De Veritate*, as quoted in Theisen (1976:21–22).

Arrupe, Pedro. "Catechesis and Inculturation." *Teaching All Nations* 15/1 (1978).

Barth, Karl. *Church Dogmatics* 1–2. ed. and trans. G. W. Bromiley and T. F. Torrance. Edinburgh: T. and T. Clark, 1956.

Baum, Gregory. "The First Papal Encyclical." *The Ecumenist* 17/4 (1979).

———. *Religion and Alienation: A Theological Reading of Sociology*. New York: Paulist Press, 1975.

Bellah, Robert. *The Broken Covenant: American Civil Religion in a Time of Trial*. New York: Seabury/Crossroad, 1975.

Belloc, Hilaire. *Europe and the Faith*. London, 1920.

Berger, Peter. *Pyramids of Sacrifice: Political Ethics and Social Change*. New York: Basic Books, 1974.

———. *A Rumor of Angels: Modern Society and the Rediscovery of the Supernatural*. New York: Doubleday/Anchor Books, 1970.

Best, Eugene C. "Grace: An Anthropological Perspective." *Journal of Ecumenical Studies* 14/2 (Spring 1977): 249–59.

Bitek, Okot p'. *African Religion in Western Scholarship*. Nairobi: East African Literature Bureau, 1970.

Bluhm, William T. *Force or Freedom: The Paradox in Modern Political Thought*. New Haven and London: Yale University Press, 1984.

Boenhoffer, Dietrich. *Life Together*. London: SCM Press, 1954.

Boff, Leonard. *Ecclesiogenesis: The Base Communities Reinvent the Church*. Trans. Robert R. Barr. Maryknoll, N.Y.: Orbis Books, 1986.

Burghardt, Walter J. "Freedom and Authority in Education." *Theology Digest* 16/4 (Winter 1968): 310–15.

Burns, J. Patout. "The Economy of Salvation: Two Patristic Traditions." In *Why the Church?*, eds. Walter J. Burghardt and William J. Thompson. New York: Paulist Press, 1976.

Camps, Arnulf. *Partners in Dialogue: Christianity and the Other World Religions*. Trans. John Drury. Maryknoll, N.Y.: Orbis Books, 1983.

The Church Teaches. Comp. by the Jesuits of St. Mary's College. St. Louis: B. Herder, 1955.

Clement of Alexandria. *Opera Quae Existant Omnia II* (Oxon 1715). *Patrologiae Graecae Tomus VII, Pars Prior*, ed. J.-P. Migne. Paris, 1857.

Clement I of Rome, Pope. *Opera Omnia I* (Oxon 1715). In *Patrologiae Graecae Tomus I*, ed. J.-P. Migne. Paris, 1857.

Congar, Yves. *Christ, Our Lady and the Church: A Study in Irenic Theology.* Trans. Henry St. John. Westminster, Md.: Newman Press, 1957.

——. *This Chruch That I Love.* Trans. Lucien Delafuente. Denville, N.J.: Dimension Books, 1965.

——. *A History of Theology.* Trans. H. Guthrie. New York: Doubleday, 1968.

Crowe, Frederick E. *Son of God, Holy Spirit and World: The Contribution of Bernard Lonergan to the Wider Ecumenism.* Toronto: Regis College, 1984.

Curran, Charles C. *Toward an American Catholic Moral Theology.* Notre Dame: University of Notre Dame Press, 1987.

Danielou, Jean. *Holy Pagans of the Old Testament.* London: Longmans, Green and Co., 1957.

D'Costa, Gavin. "John Hick's Copernican Revolution Ten Years After." *New Blackfriars* 56 (July-August 1984): 769–70.

——. *John Hick's Theology of Religion: A Critical Evaluation.* New York, London and Lanham, Md.: University Press of America, 1987.

——. "Karl Rahner's Anonymous Christian—A Reappraisal." *Modern Theology* 1/2 (January 1985): 131–48.

——. "The Pluralist Paradigm in the Christian Theology of Religions." *Scottish Journal of Theology* 39/2 (1986b): 211–24.

——. *Theology and Religious Pluralism.* Oxford: Basil Blackwell, 1986a.

Denzinger, Henry, ed. *Enchiridion Symbolorum.* 30th ed. revised by Karl Rahner; trans. Roy J. Deferrari. St. Louis: B. Herder, 1957.

Dodd, C. H. *Gospel and Law.* New York: Columbia University Press, 1951.

Driver, Tom F. "The Case for Pluralism." In *The Myth of Christian Uniqueness: Toward a Pluralistic Theology of Religions*, ed. John Hick and Paul F. Knitter. Maryknoll, N.Y.: Orbis Books, 1987.

Drummond, Richard Henry. *Toward a New Age in Christian Theology.* Maryknoll, N.Y.: Orbis Books, 1985.

Eboussi. Boulaga, F. *Christianity Without Fetishes: An African Critique and Recapture of Christianity.* Trans. Robert R. Barr. Maryknoll N.Y.: Orbis Books, 1984.

Edwards, Denis. *What Are They Saying About Salvation?* New York: Paulist Press, 1986.

England, John. "Letter to John Forsyth." In *The Works of John England* 5, ed. Sebastian G. Messmer. Cleveland: Arthur H. Clark Co., 1908.

Fitzmyer, Joseph. *Scripture and Christology: A Statement of the Biblical Commission with a Commentary.* New York: Paulist Press, 1986.

Folkemer, Lawrence D. "Dialogue and Proclamation." *Journal of Ecumenical Studies* 13/3 (Summer 1976): 420–39.

Frankena, William K. "Is Morality Logically Dependent On Religion?" In *Religion and Morality*, ed. Gene Outka and John P. Reeder, Jr. New York: Doubleday/ Anchor Books, 1973.

Freeman, Kathleen. *Ancilla To the Pre-Socratic Philosophers.* Oxford: Basil Blackwell, 1948.

Fries, Heinrich, and Johann Finsterholzl. "Infallibility." In *Sacramentum Mundi: An Encyclopedia of Theology 3*, ed. Karl Rahner. New York: Herder and Herder, 1968.

Fuchs, Josef. *Human Values and Christian Morality.* Trans. Heelan, Redmond,

Young and Watson. Dublin: Gill and Macmillan, 1970.

Fulbright, William J. *The Arrogance of Power.* New York: Random House/Vintage, 1966.

Gadamer, Hans-Georg. "Religious and Poetic Speaking." In *Myth, Symbol and Reality,* ed. Alan M. Olson. Notre Dame and London: University of Notre Dame Press, 1980.

Geertz, Clifford. *The Interpretation of Cultures.* New York: Basic Books and Harper Torchbooks, 1973.

Gellerman, Saul W. "Why 'Good' Managers Make Bad Ethical Choices." *Harvard Business Review* 86/4 (July/August 1986): 85–90.

Gilkey, Langdon. "Plurality and Its Theological Implications." In *The Myth of Christian Uniqueness: Toward a Pluralistic Theology of Religions,* ed. John Hick and Paul F. Knitter. Maryknoll, N.Y.: Orbis Books, 1987.

Gutierrez, Gustavo. *A Theology of Liberation.* Maryknoll, N.Y.: Orbis Books, 1973.

Hellwig, Monika. *Jesus the Compassion of God.* Wilmington: Michael Glazier, Inc., 1983.

Hick, John. *God Has Many Names.* Philadelphia: Westminster Press, 1980.

———. "Jesus and the World Religions." In *The Myth of God Incarnate,* ed. John Hick. London: SCM Press, 1977.

Hillman, Eugene. "Inculturation." In *The New Dictionary of Theology,* ed. Joseph A. Komonchak et al. Wilmington: Michael Glazier, Inc., 1987.

———. "Pluriformity in Ethics." *Irish Theological Quarterly* 40/3 (July 1973): 264–75.

———. *Polygamy Reconsidered: African Plural Marriage and the Christian Churches.* Maryknoll, N.Y.: Orbis Books, 1975.

———. *The Wider Ecumenism.* New York: Herder and Herder, 1968.

Houlden, J. L. *Ethics and the New Testament.* Harmondsworth: Penguin Books, 1973.

Iraeneus, St. *Contra Haereses I-III-IV* In *Patrologiae Gracae Tomus VII,* ed. J.-P. Migne. Paris, 1857.

John Paul II, Pope. *Catechesi Tradendae.* "Apostolic Constitution on Catechesis." In *Living Light* 17 (Spring 1980): 44–89.

———. *Redemptor Hominis. Acta Apostolicae Sedis* 71 (1979): 257–324.

James, E. O. *The Beginning of Religion.* London: Hutchinson-Arrow, 1958.

Justin, Martyr. "The First Apology." Trans. Thomas B. Falls. In *The Fathers of the Church: The Writings of Justin Martyr,* ed. Ludwig Schopp. New York: Christian Heritage, Inc., 1948.

Knitter, Paul F. *No Other Name? A Critical Survey of Christian Attitudes Toward the World Religions.* Maryknoll, N.Y.: Orbis Books, 1985.

——— et al. "Review Symposium." In *Horizons* 13/1 (Spring 1986): 116–35.

———. "Towards a Liberation Theology of Religions." In *The Myth of Christian Uniqueness: Toward a Pluralistic Theology of Religions,* ed. John Hick and Paul F. Knitter. Maryknoll, N.Y.: Orbis Books, 1987.

Küng, Hans, et al. *Christianity and the World Religions: Paths of Dialogue with Islam, Hinduism and Buddhism.* Trans. Peter Heinegg. New York: Doubleday, 1986.

Lane, Dermot A. *The Experience of God: An Invitation to Do Theology.* New York: Paulist Press, 1981.

———. *The Reality of Jesus.* Dublin and London: Veritas Publications; Sheed and Ward, 1975.

Leonhardt, Godfrey. "Morality and Happiness Among the Dinka." In *Religion and*

Morality, ed. Gene Outka and John P. Reeder, Jr. New York: Doubleday/Anchor Books, 1973.

Levi-Strauss, Claude. *The Scope of Anthropology.* Trans. S. O. Paul and R. A. Paul. London: Jonathan Cape, 1967.

Lonergan, Bernard. *Insight: A Study of Human Understanding.* New York: Philosophical Library, 1957.

————. *Method in Theology.* New York: Seabury, 1972.

————. *A Second Collection.* London: Darton, Longman and Todd, 1974.

Lubac, Henri de. *The Church: Paradox and Mystery.* Trans. James R. Dunne. Shannon: Ecclesia Press, 1967.

Maguire, Daniel C. *The Moral Choice.* Minneapolis: Winston Press, 1979.

McGregor, Bede. "Commentary on *Evangelii Nuntiandi.*" *Doctrine and Life.* Special Issue (March-April 1977).

McKenzie, John L. *The Civilization of Christianity.* Chicago: Thomas Moore Press, 1986.

Milhaven, John Giles. *Toward a New Catholic Morality.* New York: Doubleday, 1970.

Murphy-O'Connor, Jerome. *Becoming Human Together.* Dublin: Veritas Publications, 1978.

O'Callaghan, John J. "Reflections on Humanae Vitae." *Theology Digest* 16/4 (Winter 1968): 317-27.

O'Collins, Gerald. *Fundamental Theology.* New York: Paulist Press, 1981.

Otunga, Cardinal Maurice. "African Cultures and Life-Centered Catechesis" (Address to 1977 Synod in Rome). *African Ecclesial Review* 20/1 (February 1978).

Panikkar, Raimundo. *Myth, Faith and Hermeneutics: Cross-Cultural Studies.* New York: Paulist Press, 1979.

————. *The Unknown Christ of Hinduism: Towards an Ecumenical Christophany.* Rev. and enlarged ed. Maryknoll, N.Y.: Orbis Books, 1981.

Pannenberg, Wolfhart. *Basic Questions in Theology: Collected Essays II.* Trans. George H. Kehm. Philadelphia: Fortress Press, 1971.

Paul VI, Pope. "Discourse at All-Africa Episcopal Conference in Uganda" (31 July 1969). *Gaba Pastoral Papers*, no. 7, Symposium Dossier. Eldoret, Kenya, 48-51.

————. "Evangelization in Africa Today" (26 September 1975). *Christ to the World* 21/5 (1976); also *L'Osservatore Romano*, English ed. (9 October 1975).

————. "Evangelization in the Modern World." *Evangelii Nuntiandi* (8 December 1975). Washington, D.C.: United States Catholic Conference, 1976.

————. *Regimini Ecclesiae. Acta Apostolicae Sedis* 59 (1967).

Pawlikowski, John T. *Christ in the Light of the Christian-Jewish Dialogue.* New York: Paulist Press, 1982.

Propaganda Fidei, S. Congregationis De. *Collectanea I.* Rome: Vatican, 1907.

Race, Alan. *Christians and Religious Pluralism: Patterns in the Christian Theology of Religions.* Maryknoll, N.Y.: Orbis Books, 1985.

Rahner, Karl. "Atheism and Implicit Christianity." *Theology Digest.* Sesquicentennial Issue (February 1968): 43-56.

————. *The Christian of the Future.* Herder: Freiburg, 1967.

————. "Faith" and "Incarnation." In *Sacramentum Mundi: An Encyclopedia of Theology* 2, ed. Karl Rahner et al. New York: Herder and Herder, 1968.

————. *Foundations of Christian Faith.* Trans. William V. Dych. New York: Seabury/Crossroad, 1978.

————. *Mission and Grace 1.* London: Sheed and Ward, 1963.

———. *Nature and Grace.* London: Sheed and Ward, 1963.

———. *Theological Investigations.* Vols. 1, 4, 5, 6, 9, 10, 11, 12, 13, 14, 16, 17, 18, 20. London, Baltimore, New York, 1961–81.

Ratzinger, Joseph. *Christian Brotherhood.* Trans. W. A. Glen-Doepel. London: Sheed and Ward, 1966.

———. "A Conversation with Joseph Ratzinger." In *Faith: Conversations With Contemporary Theologians*, ed. Teofilo Cabestrero; trans. Donald D. Walsh. Maryknoll, N.Y.: Orbis Books, 1981, 147–57.

———. "Revelation Itself." In *A Commentary on the Documents of Vatican II* 3, ed. Herbert Vorgrimler. New York: Herder and Herder, 1969.

Richard, Lucien. *What Are They Saying About Christ and the World Religions?* New York: Paulist Press, 1981.

Riesenhuber, Klaus. "Rahner's 'Anonymous Christian.' " *Theology Digest* 13 (1965): 163–71.

Roman, Heinrich A. *The Natural Law.* Trans. T. R. Hanley. St. Louis and London: B. Herder, 1948.

Rossano, Pietro. "Christ's Lordship and Religious Pluralism in Roman Catholic Perspective." In *Christ's Lordship and Religious Pluralism*, ed. Gerald H. Anderson and F. Stransky. Maryknoll, N.Y.: Orbis Books, 1983.

Schillebeeckx, Edward. *Christ the Sacrament of the Encounter with God.* London: Sheed and Ward, 1963.

———. "The Church and Mankind." *Concilium* 1/1 (January 1965), British edition.

———. *Mary, Mother of the Redemption.* London: Sheed and Ward, 1964.

———. *Jesus in Our Western Culture: Mysticism, Ethics and Politics*, Trans. John Bowden. (180) London: SCM Press, 1987.

Schineller, Peter J. "Christ and the Church: A Spectrum of Views." *Theological Studies* 37/4 (1976): 545–66.

Schlette, Heinz Robert. *Towards a Theology of Religions.* Trans. W. J. O'Hare. New York: Herder and Herder, 1966.

Schreiter, Robert J. *Constructing Local Theologies.* Maryknoll, N.Y.: Orbis Books, 1985.

Schüller, Bruno. "Remarks on the Authentic Pronouncements of the Magisterium." *Theology Digest* 16/4 (Winter 1968): 328–32.

Secretariat for Non-Christians. "The Attitude of the Church Towards the Followers of Other Religions: Reflections and Orientations on Dialogue and Mission." *Bulletin: Secretariatus pro non Christianis* 56 (1984), XIX, 2. Reprint in *International Bulletin of Missionary Research* 9/4 (Oct. 1985): 187–91.

Senior, Donald, and Carroll Stuhlmueller. *The Biblical Foundations for Mission.* Maryknoll, N.Y.: Orbis Books, 1984.

Sizemore, Burlan A., Jr. "Christianity in a Pluralistic World." In *Journal of Ecumenical Studies* 13/3 (Summer 1976): 405–19.

Smith, Wilfred Cantwell. "The World Church and the World History of Religion: The Theological Issue." In Catholic Theological Society of America, *Proceedings of 39th Annual Convention*, 1984, pp. 52–68.

———. *The Faith of Other Men.* New York: Harper/Torchbooks, 1972.

———. *The Meaning and End of Religion.* New York: Harper and Row, 1978.

———. *Towards a World Theology: Faith and the Comparative History of Religion.* Philadelphia: Westminster Press, 1981.

Sobrino, Jon. *Christology at the Crossroads.* Maryknoll, N.Y.: Orbis Books, 1978.

Stransky, Thomas F. "The Declaration on Non-Christian Religions." In *Vatican II: An Interfaith Appraisal*, ed. John H. Miller. Notre Dame and London: University of Notre Dame Press, 1966, 335–48.

Theisen, Jerome P. *The Ultimate Church and the Promise of Salvation.* Collegeville, Minn. St. John's University Press, 1976.

Thompson, William M. "The Risen Christ, Transcultural Consciousness, and the Encounter of the World Religions." In *Theological Studies* 37/3 (1976): 381–401.

Tillich, Paul. "Missions and World History." In *The Theology of the Christian Mission.* ed. G. H. Anderson. London: SCM Press, 1961.

Toynbee, Arnold. *Christianity Among the Religions of the World.* New York: Scribner, 1957.

———. *An Historian's Approach to Religion.* New York: Oxford University Press, 1956.

Tracy, David. *The Analogical Imagination: Christian Theology and the Culture of Pluralism.* New York: Crossroads, 1981.

Troeltsch, Ernst. *Christian Thought.* London: London University Press, 1923.

Tuchman, Barbara A. *The March of Folly from Troy to Vietnam.* New York: Ballantine Books, 1984.

Vatican Council II. *Documents of Vatican II*, ed. Austin P. Flannery. Grand Rapids, Mich.: William B. Eerdmans Publishing Co., 1975.

Vorgrimler, Herbert. *Understanding Karl Rahner: An Introduction to His Life and Thought.* New York: Crossroad, 1968.

Index

Orbis' Faith Meets Faith Series

THE SILENCE OF GOD: THE ANSWER OF THE BUDDHA

by Raimundo Panikkar

With his deep knowledge of Indian thought and his special ability to explicate Buddhist texts and tenets, Panikkar analyzes issues of Budddist-Christian dialogue effectively from *both* the Christian and the Buddhist perspectives. *The Silence of God* explores the radical difference between the Christian concept of God and that of Buddhism, challenging the Western view of Buddhism as "atheistic" and searching for the meaning of God beyond the traditional theories. Panikkar seeks a way "to purify all our notions of a Mystery which seems to elude any experience yet which cannot be erased from human consciousness."

"A remarkable, helpful, and most challenging book." *—Harold Coward*

400pp. Notes, bibliography, indexes.

ISBN 0-88344-445-3 Paper   0-88344-446-1 Cloth

LOVE MEETS WISDOM

A Christian Experience of Buddhism

by Aloysius Pieris, S.J.

Using the framework of a pluralistic theology of religions, Pieris explores the social as well as the spiritual dimensions of Buddhism, its doctrine and political vision, and issues related to Buddhist-Christian understanding.

160pp.

ISBN 0-88344-371-6 Paper   0-88344-372-4 Cloth

THE DIALOGICAL IMPERATIVE

A Christian Reflection on Interfaith Encounter

by David Lochhead

Offering a concise treatment of the nature and goals of interfaith dialogue, Lochhead defines and affirms the dialogical approach from within the Reformed Protestant tradition.

"An uncommonly wise and helpful book. . . ." *—Schubert M. Ogden*

120pp. Notes, index.

ISBN 0-88344-611-1 Paper   0-88344-612-X Cloth

AN ASIAN THEOLOGY OF LIBERATION

by Aloysius Pieris, S.J.

The eminent Sri Lankan theologian discusses topics critical to Christianity in Asia and beyond: inculturation, poverty, spirituality, mission, and ideology.

"It is the challenge of Aloysius Pieris that he seeks to trace the search for grace in Asian flesh and to articulate it in an Asian idiom. His voice deserves to be heard, his message pondered." *—William McConville*

200pp. Bibliography, index.

ISBN 0-88344-626-X Paper   0-88344-627-8 Cloth

THE MYTH OF CHRISTIAN UNIQUENESS
Toward a Pluralistic Theology of Religions
Edited by John Hick and Paul F. Knitter
A widely representative assembly of Christian theologians explore the meaning and consequences of the pluralistic model for Christianity. Contributors include Gordon C. Kaufman, Langdon Gilkey, Wilfred Cantwell Smith, Stanley J. Samartha, Raimundo Panikkar, Seiichi Yagi, Rosemary Radford Ruether, Marjorie Hewitt Suchocki, Aloysius Pieris, Tom F. Driver.
"An important study of what is fast becoming the central issue of contemporary Christian self-understanding." — *David Tracy*
240pp. Index.
ISBN 0-88344-602-2 Paper   0-88344-603-0 Cloth

TOWARD A UNIVERSAL THEOLOGY OF RELIGION
Edited by Leonard Swidler
Original essays by Hans Küng, Wilfred Cantwell Smith, John Cobb, and Raimundo Panikkar elicit responses from world theologians, resulting in a dialogue that squarely faces the challenges of a universal theology of religion. Contributors include Kana Mitra, Stanley S. Harakas, Zalman Schachter, Kenneth K. Inada, Antony Fernando, Charles Wei-Hsun Fu, Thomas Dean, Bibhuti S. Yadav, Khalid Duran, and Ellen Zubrack Charry.
"An important confrontation ... on a topic that is of the utmost urgency. ..."
—Jan Van Bragt
264pp.
ISBN 0-88344-555-7 Paper   0-88344-580-8 Cloth

Of Related Interest

TOWARDS A WORLD THEOLOGY
Faith and the Comparative History of Religion
by Wilfred Cantwell Smith
Arguing the need to use the data of comparative religion as the basis for a world theology, Smith searches for a new language of a global theology that does justice both to the universal quality of faith and to the particular faith traditions that are the context of religious life.
206pp.
ISBN 0-88344-646-4 Paper

THE BIBLE AND PEOPLE OF OTHER FAITHS
by S. Wesley Ariarajah
Ariarajah shows how the Bible cannot be used as "a dividing wall" but is instead "the lamp that sheds light on the life of Christians as they seek to live ... with people of other faiths."
88pp.
ISBN 0-88344-272-8 Paper

DISPUTED QUESTIONS
On Being a Christian
by Rosemary Radford Ruether
What does it mean to be a Roman Catholic, a woman, an American, educated and

middle-class, in an unjust world? Ruether autobiographically charts her personal odyssey of faith and identity, leading to a theology that rejects exclusivism, confronts racism and sexism, and embraces human pluralism.
142pp.
ISBN 0-88344-549-2 Paper

SACRED WORD AND SACRED TEXT
Scripture in World Religions
by Harold Coward
A fascinating exploration of the oral as well as the written tradition of scripture in Judaism, Christianity, Islam, Hinduism, Sikhism, and Buddhism.
"Coward's book is Comparative Religion at its best. . . . He strikes a harmonious balance between the power of the oral and that of the written tradition not only for the past but also for the present."—*Raimundo Panikkar*
232pp. Notes, index.
ISBN 0-88344-604-9 Paper   0-88344-605-7 Cloth

PLURALISM
Challenge to World Religions
by Harold Coward
A comprehensive treatment of how Judaism, Christianity, Islam, Hinduism, and Buddhism have understood their particular claim to absolute truth in the face of the truth claims of other religions.
"Here is a valuable new resource. . . . For the first time we have a clear and systematic account of the attitudes of each of the great world religions to the others."
—*John Hick*
164pp. Notes, index.
ISBN 0-88344-710-X Paper

Liberation Theology

INTRODUCING LIBERATION THEOLOGY
by Leonardo Boff and Clodovis Boff
Two of Latin America's leading Catholic theologians have written this introductory-level book for the person who asks, "What is liberation theology?" Meticulous organization and forceful presentation make this text, as Robert F. Drinan says, "one of the finest explanations of liberation theology in the English language."
112pp. Bibliography.
ISBN 0-88344-550-6 Paper   0-88344-575-1 Cloth

A THEOLOGY OF LIBERATION
Fifteenth Anniversary Edition
Gustavo Gutiérrez
Revision of the book which more than any other has focused and directed the world-wide discussion of liberation theology. A substantial new introduction reviews the evolution, current status, and key themes for the future.
312pp. Notes, indexes.
ISBN 0-88344-542-5 Paper   0-88344-543-3 Cloth

THIRD WORLD LIBERATION THEOLOGIES
An Introductory Survey
THIRD WORLD LIBERATION THEOLOGIES
A Reader
Deane William Ferm
Valuable introductions to liberation theologians and their basic writings. The *Survey* is a thorough, compact review of liberation theology via concise portraits of its major figures from Latin America, Africa, and Asia. The *Reader* offers 27 selections that demonstrate the rich variety of liberation thought and scholarship. "Excellent for classes at the church, college, and seminary levels."
— The Christian Century
Survey 160pp. Notes, bibliography, index.
ISBN 0-88344-515-8 Paper
Reader 400pp. Notes.
ISBN 0-88344-516-6 Paper

Ethics

CATHOLIC SOCIAL TEACHING
Our Best-Kept Secret
by Peter Henriot, Edward De Berri, Michael Schultheis
A compact outline of the major Catholic documents on social issues, including "On Social Concerns" (1988).
94pp. Notes, bibliography, study guide.
ISBN 0-88344-632-4 Paper

CHRISTIAN ETHICS
A Case Method Approach
Robert L. Stivers, Christine E. Gudorf, Alice Frazer Evans, and Robert A. Evans, editors
Sixteen cases, on business and economics, health and medicine, life and death, underscore the importance of a Christian ethical outlook in facing the pressing dilemmas of our time. Includes an Appendix on teaching by use of the case method approach.
288pp.
ISBN 0-88344-424-0 Paper

ETHICS AND LIBERATION
An Introduction
by Charles L. Kammer, III
Exploring both the strengths and weaknesses of traditional Christian ethics, Kammer proposes a transition to ethics of *theonomous* responsibility, based on the precepts of liberation theology.
"All the elements of a Christian ethic are here in an amazingly compact presentation." *—Larry L. Rasmussen*
272pp. Notes, index.
ISBN 0-88344-608-1 Paper